# TEN-MINUTE PLAYS: VOLUME 5
## FROM

## THEATRE OF LOUISVILLE

D0596019

Edited by

**Michael Bigelow Dixon** and **Amy Wegener**

With a Foreword by **Jon Jory**

A SAMUEL FRENCH ACTING EDITION

SAMUEL FRENCH
FOUNDED 1830

SAMUELFRENCH.COM

**ISBN 978-0-573-62701-0**　　　　Printed in U.S.A.　　　　#22275

**IMPORTANT BILLING AND CREDIT REQUIREMENTS**

All producers of any play in this volume *must* give credit to the Author of the Play in all programs distributed in connection with performances of the Play and in all instances in which the title of the Play appears for purposes of advertising, publicizing or otherwise exploiting the Play and/or a production. The name of the Author *must* also appear on a separate line, on which no other name appears, immediately above the title, and *must* appear in size of type not less than fifty percent the size of the title type.

# FOREWORD

Twenty-five years ago, Actors Theatre of Louisville started experimenting with this odd, cranky, demanding, harder-than-you'd-think, fascinating form: the ten-minute play. As I remember, it served two masters for us. First, we were holding annual one-act play festivals, and this was a way to attract writers who might not otherwise have time for us; and second, we were frustrated that there were so few age-specific pieces for actors in their twenties. Out of these practical concerns (necessity *still* being the mother of invention) grew a quarter-century-long, institutional obsession that focused more and more on the values and challenges of the form and less and less on the simple problem-solving. We certainly didn't invent it, but we are proud to have adopted it in its infancy and parented it into its current maturity.

The ten-minute play, as you have doubtless noticed, is here, it's there, it's literally everywhere (at least eleven foreign countries that we know of)! What's the perfume that makes it so attractive? Certainly its intensity and, like miniaturist art and haiku, its surprising complexity, plus (let's face it) its ... well ... brevity. Length being a relativist perception, however, in this age of the ten-second sound bite, these plays are pretty long.

So here it is, a fifth volume with plays you can do in a car, a room, under a bridge or even in a theatre. The authors include William Mastrosimone, Jane Martin, Thomas Babe, Richard Dresser and Elizabeth Wong, along with a whole new generation of writers you need to get to know. Most of these plays come to us via our National Ten-Minute Play Contest, but the form's sneaky (one play arrived in an empty cereal box). If you find a new use for them we don't know about, drop us a note ... but make sure it's not more than ten pages long.

**Jon Jory**
**Producing Director**
**Actors Theatre of Louisville**

## ABOUT ACTORS THEATRE OF LOUISVILLE

The 1998-99 season at Actors Theatre of Louisville marked a double celebration for the world-renowned nonprofit stage company—the theatre's 35th birthday and Jon Jory's 30th anniversary as Producing Director. Under Mr. Jory's leadership, Actors Theatre has emerged as one of America's most consistently innovative professional theatre companies. For over 20 years it has been a major force in revitalizing American playwriting with nearly 300 ATL-premiered scripts already in publication.

ATL's annual Humana Festival of New American Plays is recognized as the premiere event of its kind and draws producers, journalists, critics, playwrights and theatre lovers from around the world for a marathon of new works. More than 250 Humana Festival plays have been added to the active American repertoire. The biennial Bingham Signature Shakespeare Series offers Louisville the best of the Bard on an uncompromised production level, which only a handful of cities can achieve.

Actors Theatre, designated the State Theatre of Kentucky, is distinguished as one of the few regional companies in the country which operates three diverse theatres under one roof: the 637-seat Pamela Brown Auditorium, the 318-seat Bingham Theatre and the 159-seat Victor Jory Theatre. Its programming includes a broad range of classical and contemporary work, presenting over 600 performances in a year-round season. Each play is directed and produced in Louisville with the costumes, scenery and properties seen on stage made by ATL's professional staff.

Actors Theatre performs annually to over 200,000 people and is the recipient of the most prestigious awards bestowed on a regional theatre: a special Tony Award for Distinguished Achievement, the James N. Vaughan Memorial Award for Exceptional Achievement and Contribution to the Development of Professional Theatre, and the Margo Jones Award for the Encouragement of New Plays. Actors Theatre's international appearances include performances in over 29 cities in 15 foreign countries.

# TABLE OF CONTENTS

# ACKNOWLEDGEMENTS

In addition to all the playwrights whose plays are featured in this book, and the excellent staff at Samuel French, the editors wish to thank the following persons for their invaluable assistance in compiling this volume:

Erica Blumfield
Ilana Brownstein
Andrea Whitley Clark
Preston Dyches
Jim Gastinger
Adrien-Alice Hansel
Sara Kmack
Kelly Lea Miller
Laura Grace Pattillo
Jeffrey Rodgers
Sara Skolnick
Alexander Speer

AND

Charmaine Ferenczi
Jason Fogelson
Robert Freedman
Mary Harden
Ronald Gwiazda
Joyce Ketay
George Lane

# SINGLETON, THE MEDAL WINNER

by

## Thomas Babe

## SINGLETON, THE MEDAL WINNER
### by Thomas Babe

Directed by Stuart Carden
Dramaturg: Megan Shultz

*Chubbs:* Craig Michael Robillard
*Singleton:* Erich Hamm
*Davis/Voice:* Adam Montgomery Richman

Scenic Designer: Tom Burch
Costume Designer: Emily McConnell
Lighting Designer: Paul Werner
Sound Designer: Mark Huang
Properties Designer: Mark Walston
Stage Manager: Jennifer Wills
Assistant Stage Managers: Patty Thoreson, Laura Jean Wickman

## CHARACTERS

Chubbs, the surgeon, 20s

Singleton, the soldier, 20s

Davis and The Voice, both 20s (Same actor)

## TIME

1863

# SINGLETON, THE MEDAL WINNER

## Scene 1

*(A Civil War vintage Union flag upstage. Downstage, SINGLE-TON, the wounded soldier, suspended on a plank tilted toward us from a giant scales. The arrow on the face of the scales reads—144 pounds. Nearby, in a bloody coat and holding a brown bottle and spoon, is the surgeon, CHUBBS.)*

SINGLETON. Can you save me?

CHUBBS. I can do my best. But not how you were. Not in one piece. The leg will have to go. It is your *vulni lutulici.* Also ... I fear you have contracted erysipelas. Take it how you will—you've lost nearly all the meat on your body.

*(Steamboat whistle sounds quite near.)*

SINGLETON. Can you make my pain, though, stand its distance? *(CHUBBS gets up, pours brown liquid into the spoon and ladles it down SINGLETON's throat. SINGLETON smacks his lips.)* That's whiskey—is all that is.

CHUBBS. That's all I know that works anymore.

*(Steamboat whistle again.)*

SINGLETON. We're taking on ice.

CHUBBS. That's right. That's very good.

SINGLETON. The blocks'll be sliding down right under us. *(Imitating the sounds.)* Shirrr-skissss-bonk! Shirrr-skisss-bonk! Last time, or time before last, Nurse McInerney was saying, one block cut loose and smashed open three coffins. *(Pause.)* When I'm to be buried on the shore, leave a barrel stave stuck in the mud with my name on it. In ink. So the boys can find me and take me home.

11

CHUBBS. They won't want you like that—thin and in the ground for weeks.

SINGLETON. They won't care.

CHUBBS. You're going to make it.

SINGLETON. No.

CHUBBS. You're going to make it.

SINGLETON. No. You have me on the weighing machine.

CHUBBS. You don't know why I have you on the weighing machine.

SINGLETON. To measure when my soul flees.

CHUBBS. I am a surgeon. You can't know half what I know. Don't make me despise you.

*(CAPTAIN DAVIS, in a well-traveled uniform, comes in.)*

CHUBBS. Yes?

DAVIS. I am here to arrange presentation to ... *(Looks at his papers.)* ... Joseph Singleton—of his medal.

SINGLETON. For what?

DAVIS. I don't know. Don't you know?

SINGLETON. No.

DAVIS. *(To CHUBBS.)* Can I do this in about one hour?

CHUBBS. Give him the medal now.

DAVIS. I don't have it. They're taking it on. With the other supplies.

SINGLETON. And the ice. Shirr-skiss-bonk. Where does the ice come from? Do you know where the ice comes from? In this heat, where do they find it?

DAVIS. I don't know.

CHUBBS. It's stored up to the North.

*(Sound of the ice beneath. Shirr-skiss-bonk. Shirr-skiss-bonk.)*

SINGLETON. Can you get me a sliver of ice, please, to wet my lips with?

*(CHUBBS and DAVIS look at each other. Blackout.)*

## Scene 2

*(SINGLETON sits by himself, his rifle upright under his arm. He has one boot off and is thoughtfully picking at his toes.)*

SINGLETON. *(Calling softly.)* Where you at?

MAN's VOICE. Where I was.

SINGLETON. Should I come over?

MAN's VOICE. Can you reach me?

SINGLETON. I can do my best. What's here between us?

MAN's VOICE. Where they shoot so well.

SINGLETON. Sharper's Alley. Would you be the one, then, doing all the bushwacking?

MAN's VOICE. I'm hungry.

SINGLETON. I'll be right over. I've got cartridges here and some biscuits and bacon. I put a gun to the quartermaster's son-of-a-bitching head. All the men are hungry, I told him. All the men are sick and tired and hungry.

MAN's VOICE. I'm thirsty.

SINGLETON. That's okay, too. I got a block of ice.

*(Very distant steamboat whistle.)*

MAN's VOICE. Where's ice come from this time of year?

SINGLETON. From a polar bear's mansion to the North. *(Pause.)* You have a fever?

MAN's VOICE. Like lightning in my chest.

SINGLETON. I have lice. And I cut myself in the hand paring an apple at Gettysburg. My *vulni lutulici. (Pause.)* And I have something wrong in the middle of me. Below the middle of me. It's hard and sore.

MAN's VOICE. Leave off talking about it.

*(SINGLETON puts on his boot and stands up.)*

SINGLETON. Hard and sore and hot ... and, I don't recall what else. Well, I'm coming over.

MAN's VOICE. You want to die?

SINGLETON. I want to be over there—with you.

MAN's VOICE. You don't really have no food.

SINGLETON. Some.

MAN's VOICE. No cartridges.

SINGLETON. Some.

MAN's VOICE. No cake of ice.

SINGLETON. No. But I thought of a cake of ice.

MAN's VOICE. You *do* want to die.

SINGLETON. No, I don't want to die. I want to nearly die. But first, I want to be over there with you. So you will remember me.

Forever. Till you are extinguished by some shot or shell. My name is Joseph Singleton.

MAN's VOICE. Joseph Singleton. Your face sounds like another face I heard just recently.

SINGLETON. You've never pictured my face.

MAN's VOICE. In a polar bear's mansion.

*(Laughs harshly.)*

SINGLETON. I'm having trouble with you. Tell me, then. Are you fair? Or are you dark? Short? Tall? Disfigured somewise? Do you sport calluses on your hands?

MAN's VOICE. I was a blacksmith once. I sport calluses on my hands.

SINGLETON. Good. Now—how much do you weigh?

MAN's VOICE. Less.

SINGLETON. I weigh more. I used to be a feather. But lately, I've been feasting on bits of the men I've killed.

MAN's VOICE. You never killed nobody.

SINGLETON. I thought about it though. That made me fat.

MAN's VOICE. I despise you.

SINGLETON. Ah, but .... Didn't we love each other once? Wasn't that the purpose? Didn't I court you under your window— and you threw me down the toy soldier you had guarding Mister Lincoln in his white mansion made of ice.

MAN's VOICE. I threw you down a horse ball.

SINGLETON. Well, I caught it, then, and saved it—as I did our first kiss.

MAN's VOICE. I didn't know you ever.

*(Distant steamboat whistle.)*

SINGLETON. We begun in the glory days, when I carried the flag and I never wavered for an instant because I was good—and my heart was high and true. I did it all for you, and now you despise me. But some good will come of it still. Of all this death and pig-smell. All this endless pig-smell I find all over myself. So ... *(Pause.)* If I crawl across on my belly, I won't be but rump-shot. If I slip up and put my leg in the air, they'll take that. But, if perchance my head should rise—it'd blow up like a cantaloupe. All them many risks I'd take just to see the sweet face of my enemy.

MAN's VOICE. Go shit and fall in it.

*(Distant steamboat whistle.)*

SINGLETON. *(Taking the first step.)* They might even give me a medal, you know.

MAN's VOICE. DON'T COME HERE!

SINGLETON. *(Taking another step.)* But I bring you a sliver of ice—for your fevered lips.

MAN's VOICE. DON'T COME HERE, I SAY!

*(Gunshot nearby. Then the distant steamboat whistle.)*

SINGLETON. Hello? *(Pause.)* Hello? *(Pause.)* Son of a bitch! He shot himself!

*(SINGLETON cocks his rifle and points it directly into his own leg. He squints his eyes shut. As he is pulling the trigger ... Blackout—and in the blackout, a gunshot.)*

### Scene 3

*(The flag, the plank bed and scales. SINGLETON, asleep. CHUBBS sits, holding his hand.)*

CHUBBS. I do despise you, you know—you and your sort. The rest of them applaud you. Your courage and manhood as depicted in the newspapers. And in many a vacant bed from here to Utica, the lonely maidens rub their underbellies and moan. They're thinking of you, soldier, not of me. No one ever thinks of me.

*(SINGLETON suddenly squeezes CHUBBS's hand very hard and opens his eyes.)*

SINGLETON. You mustn't be bitter.

CHUBBS. I'm sorry. There are so many of you—and so little I know how to do.

SINGLETON. Make your heart cold, then.

CHUBBS. I do the best I can. *(Pause.)* Whiskey?

SINGLETON. Yes, thank you. *(CHUBBS doses SINGLETON.)* I know you do the best you can. I know that in my heart.

CHUBBS. Thank you. *(Pause.)* Tell me about the war, then, about your brave adventures—the adventures you, yourself, may not have seen as brave.

SINGLETON. Oh, it wasn't much. I was a toy soldier. I played in the scorching heat as I used to romp with my friends in the snow. Some of them died. I wanted some of them to die—so I could live longer. *(Looking up.)* How much do I weigh now?

CHUBBS. About the same.

SINGLETON. How much will I weigh after?

CHUBBS. I don't know. A little less, perhaps.

SINGLETON. Doctor, you are pining.

CHUBBS. I am not pining.

SINGLETON. Oh, but you are. Tell me, what are you pining for?

CHUBBS. Whole men. Winter. A ripe juicy peach. The humdrum. What are you pining for, soldier?

SINGLETON. Nothing. I've had all I could stand of every last thing I could ever want. *(Pause.)* One other item—that bit of ice I asked for?

CHUBBS. I had it here. You fell asleep. It melted. I can get you another.

SINGLETON. You needn't worry.

*(SINGLETON closes his eyes again. CHUBBS drops his head into his hands. CAPTAIN DAVIS comes in, with a grand little velvet box.)*

DAVIS. I have his medal now—and the citation. For unaccountable bravery in attacking and subduing a concentration of hostile sharpshooters. Wake him up. We'll get it done.

CHUBBS. He just passed.

DAVIS. Oh ...

*(CHUBBS wipes his eyes and gets up. He looks at the scales and makes a note on his chart.)*

CHUBBS. His soul weighed about the same as the rest.

DAVIS. Does that surprise you?

CHUBBS. I thought it would weigh more.

DAVIS. When you pack him in ice, put the medal in there with him, would you?

*(DAVIS hands the box to CHUBBS. Then he salutes the corpse of SINGLETON. And exits. CHUBBS opens the box and takes out the medal. He puts the medal—on its brilliant purple ribbon— around his own neck. Then he kisses SINGLETON on the forehead, and sits down. He takes SINGLETON's hand. Blackout.)*

**END OF PLAY**

# THE PRICE

by

## Shem Bitterman

## THE PRICE
### by Shem Bitterman

Directed by Sandra Grand
Dramaturg: Abby Weintraub

*He:*  Andrew Ritter
*She:*  Gina Giambrone

Stage Manager: Megan L. Kelly
Assistant Stage Manager: Omar Kamal
Costume Designer: Kevin R. McLeod
Lighting Designers: Michele Gallenstein, Brian Shippey
Sound Designer: Shane Rettig
Properties Designer: Mark Walston

## CHARACTERS

He
She

## SETTING

A park bench

## THE PRICE

*(A park at night.*
*A man and a woman on a bench.)*

HE. So ... anyway ... what were you saying ...?

SHE. You weren't listening?

HE. No. I was. I was listening. I was just—

SHE. What?

HE. Thinking. I'm sorry. Go on. You were saying something about your mother.

SHE. I was talking about depression.

HE. Oh, yeah. That's right. Your dad.

SHE. Nothing. Anyway. It's boring.

HE. No. I'm interested. I didn't know it was chemical. I really didn't. I suffer from depression.

SHE. Really.

HE. Maybe not as bad as your dad.

SHE. He's not so bad really ...

HE. With me it comes more suddenly. I'm happy, then—for no reason—

SHE. That's the way it is with him.

HE. What? Oh. Yeah. But I don't think of it as chemical.

SHE. You should have it looked into ...

HE. Oh. Yeah. You're right. I will. I'm sorry.

SHE. What?

HE. Did you say something?

SHE. No.

HE. Oh. Sorry.

SHE. Why do you keep apologizing?

HE. I keep getting it wrong, don't I?

SHE. Getting what wrong?

HE. This date.

SHE. It's all right.

HE. Not really. For you maybe it's all right. You don't have to wake up with yourself.

SHE. I don't?

HE. I'm sorry. Of course you have to wake up with yourself ... what I meant to say is—you don't have to wake up with *me*.

SHE. What if I wanted to?

HE. What?

SHE. To wake up with you ...

HE. Oh. Yeah. Well.

*(Pause.)*

SHE. Would you like that?

HE. Yeah. Yeah. I think that's why I've been talking so much. I'm not generally such a—

*(She leans in.)*

HE. Stop.

SHE. What?

HE. Think about what you're about to do. What I'm about to— Can we talk?

SHE. Sure. I thought that's what we were doing.

HE. Tell me about your father.

SHE. He's a nice man. We're not so close anymore.

HE. Why?

SHE. Why? I suppose ... I suppose I got tired of being the family arbitrator. The one sane person in my family. You know.

HE. Yeah. I used to have to nurse my mother through migraines.

SHE. So you know.

HE. Oh, yeah. She had a mattress on the floor. No bed. And I used to sit on the edge of it and talk her through them. Like a pilot landing a plane ...

SHE. That's how it was in my family too. Except I had two planes to land. Simultaneously.

HE. Yeah. *(Pause.)* Anyway, I'm glad you answered my ad.

SHE. Did you get a lot of response?

HE. A considerable amount.

SHE. What's considerable?

HE. Twenty.

SHE. Wow.

HE. It seemed like a lot to me too.

SHE. So what number am I?

HE. What?

SHE. In the hierarchy? Am I your first choice? Your second?

HE. Oh, no. It doesn't work like that. I agreed to meet them all.

SHE. Really? And am I the last?

HE. No.

SHE. I see.

HE. Do you answer these ads often?

SHE. Once in a while—when I have nothing better to do.

HE. Oh.

SHE. No, I'm kidding. You're my first.

HE. Really?

SHE. Yeah. Really.

HE. Wow. I mean—wow.

SHE. Well, it's just the way it worked out ... you don't have to be as flattered as all that.

HE. No, I—I'm not. I mean—I am.

SHE. Your ad did catch my attention.

HE. What about it?

SHE. I don't know. You sounded—serious—fun-loving—bright—committed—sensual—

HE. Yeah. I am those things.

SHE. It seemed a little schizophrenic to me. A little like a dog who was running in too many directions. I decided to check it out.

HE. I'm glad.

SHE. Are you?

HE. Yeah. I am. I'm glad. I liked your letter.

SHE. Did you?

HE. Yeah. I did. It was very—to the point. Very matter of fact. I appreciate that.

SHE. I'm glad.

*(Pause.)*

HE. So ... how long has it been since you've been seeing someone?

SHE. A few months.

HE. What, like ten?

SHE. More like five.

HE. Five?

SHE. Does that seem like a long time?

HE. No ... no.

SHE. I see.

HE. No. Not at all. Five isn't long at all ... especially after ... God, how long was your last relationship? You said in your letter, but I—

SHE. Five years.

HE. Wow.

SHE. Is that long?

HE. No! No. You weren't married?

SHE. No.

HE. No thought of it, or—am I getting too personal?

SHE. No. No thought of it. No. Just—didn't seem right.

HE. Yeah. That's rough ...

SHE. It was both of our decision ...

HE. Yeah. Well—

SHE. Just—

HE. Sure.

*(Pause.)*

SHE. What about you?

HE. Oh, I—uh. I was in a relationship.

SHE. Long?

HE. Some time.

SHE. How long?

HE. Some time.

SHE. Am I—?

HE. No. It was—five years.

SHE. Wow. *(HE shrugs.)* How did it end?

HE. I—ended it. Didn't seem to have a future. I wasn't ready ...

SHE. But your ad said—

HE. Yeah, well—things change ...

SHE. How long since you ... ?

HE. Five months ... like you.

SHE. Wow. Coincidence.

HE. Yeah.

*(Pause.)*

SHE. So—it's getting late.

HE. Yeah. I guess I should be getting you home.

SHE. No, I can—

HE. Oh, you want to—?

SHE. Well, it's a long trip uptown.

HE. I can—help you get a cab.

SHE. That's okay. I mean—thanks—sure. That sounds good.

HE. Look, I didn't mean to imply anything about your relationship ...

SHE. No, no—I didn't take it that way.

HE. It's just—with me—with Rachel ... that was her name—Rachel ... with Rachel and me ... it just didn't work out ... she just wasn't what I wanted ... you know ... in the long run.

SHE. You were with her for five years.

HE. That's right.

SHE. Seems like—

HE. What ... ?

SHE. I don't know. It's none of my business.

HE. Sure it is ...

SHE. Seems like it took you an awful long time to find out.

HE. Oh.

SHE. Well, if I've—

HE. No. No. No. You're right. You're right to say what you said ... it's true ... I did at first think we'd—well, anyway—look at you.

SHE. Sure, I'm no different really.

HE. That's what I'm saying—we're neither of us any different, really.

SHE. So.

HE. Yeah.

SHE. Anyway.

HE. Yeah. No. Wait. I—I like you. I thought—you know—we were closer before. Did I say anything?

SHE. No.

HE. Oh. Okay. See the thing was—with Rachel—the thing was—with her—I just didn't—I just never—that is—I—well, I really wanted, I guess I wanted it to work out for a long time ... maybe not at the very beginning ... maybe not then ... maybe I was just thinking of her as—I don't know—maybe I was just looking at her body—cause she was—well, anyway—she was very pretty... and we—it was a lark—you know—we went out to dinner—and we sat in a park ... like this, you know—warm summer night—and all—and we just—I don't know—I guess we just wanted to—both of us—I mean it wasn't like I forced her or anything—we must have just both of us wanted—to kiss—you know ... and so we did. And then we went to a movie. And then we went home. To my place. But we didn't—I mean, not that first night. Just fooled around. It was fun. We had a good time ... we played a game ... like—who would make the other—you know. Anyway—we did it, and—and, I don't know—things fell together ... they were never that great ... just—we liked each other—and I put it off to youth—you know—how confusing it all was—our feelings—and I said to her one time ... when we were at the old World Trade Center in Montreal ... I said ... If we stay together like this—for long enough—we'll get married. See. We'd invest the time and after we'd invested the time—all that time—that would become our love—see—?

SHE. I have to—

HE. Oh, I'm sorry—I—I've been talking. I'm sorry. It's late.

SHE. No, go on.

HE. I didn't mean to ...

SHE. Anyway, go on. Go on, please ...

HE. There's nothing more ... It's just ... the thought ... anyway...

SHE. What thought?

HE. Somehow, when we'd kissed ... in that park ... it was like a contract. It was fun ... It didn't mean anything. On one side ... but on the other side ... it was like the price ... you know ... the price of doing it. The price of kissing her ... was five years ... 'cause in the end ... we never really were right for one another ...

SHE. Do you believe that?

HE. I don't know.

SHE. Do you miss her?

HE. Yes.

SHE. So maybe it worked ... all those years ... the kiss, the night you spent together ... it all added up to something.

HE. But see ... from the start ... I don't know. I don't know what I ever really thought of her. I know one thing. I could never say I loved her. Never. We kissed ... and we were together for five years. It was just like that. Do you know what I mean?

SHE. The novelty wore off—

HE. No. The obligation ... the obligation that came out of the promise ... of that first kiss ... We could have just said good-night.

SHE. One of those either/or situations, huh?

HE. Yeah. I guess.

SHE. Good-night—

HE. Do you want me to—?

SHE. No, that's okay.

HE. Hey, listen—maybe another time—we can get together.

SHE. Call me.

HE. Do you mean that?

SHE. Not really.

HE. Good-bye then.

*(SHE goes.)*

HE. I'm sorry about your dad.

**END OF PLAY**

# ROADTRIP

by

## Victoria Norman Brown

## ROADTRIP
### by Victoria Norman Brown

Directed by Jeanine DeFalco
Dramaturg: Meghan Davis

*Julie*: Sarah J. Gavitt
*Dave:* Coleman Bigelow

Stage Manager: Megan L. Kelly
Assistant Stage Manager: Omar Kamal
Costume Designer: Kevin R. McLeod
Lighting Designers: Michele Gallenstein, Brian Shippey
Sound Designer: Shane Rettig
Properties Designer: Mark Walston

### CHARACTERS

JULIE, young woman
DAVE, young man

### TIME

Present

### PLACE

In a car on a U.S. interstate

# ROADTRIP

*(Young girl and young man, JULIE and DAVE in a car, driving down the road. She's driving. He rides beside her.)*

DAVE. Happy anniversary!

JULIE. What?

DAVE. It just occurred to me that we've been going out for exactly ten months today. So happy *(Leans over and kisses her on the cheek.)* anniversary.

JULIE. Not while I'm driving.

DAVE. Sorry.

JULIE. That's okay.

DAVE. Listen, Julie ...

JULIE. *(Sings.)* "Over the river and through the woods" ... no. Over the river and down 65 to Dave's parent's house we go. *(Stops singing.)* Not funny?

DAVE. You're very funny.

JULIE. Not really, but that's okay. I used to worry about being overly morose, depressed, you know—crazy. I mean, who would want a suicidal, potentially homicidal girlfriend? But then I met you and oh well.

DAVE. You're all right.

JULIE. Now, I feel great ...

DAVE. You look great.

JULIE. ... maybe don't look so hot. If I was standing, you'd see it—the culmination of two weeks of lunchtime desserts—midday too, when someone had a birthday. All that sugar and cream just sitting below my waistline. Chocolate chip cheesecake, turn-your-tongue-blue frosting—the fat content of three Big Macs each! Nerves I guess.

DAVE. My parents are going to love you.

JULIE. Just hope they don't think I'm pregnant.

DAVE. Listen, Julie, about my parents ...

JULIE. They are expecting me, aren't they?

DAVE. Yeah, they're expecting you ...

JULIE. And you told them about me—not everything, I hope. But the good things. Like I went to law school and that I'm the youngest person and the fifth woman attorney to be hired by my firm—one of the best in the city. I've traveled Europe, although I can't speak a bit of French. I hope you didn't tell them that. I've got my own place. Not as nice as I'd like. Student loans—well, you know. We don't live together ...

*(JULIE gasps.)*

DAVE. Julie ...

JULIE. That's it, isn't it? They think I'm a slut, right? Just because I answered the phone that time at your place ...

DAVE. What are you talking ...

JULIE. About a week ago. Your mom called to ask if you wanted her to make a roast beef for Thanksgiving ...

DAVE. You never told me ...

JULIE. "I doubt it," I said. "Dave's a vegetarian."

DAVE. Turkey's fine.

JULIE. "Turkey's fine." That's what I said.

| DAVE. | JULIE. |
|---|---|
| My parents aren't exactly rich, you know. | I never really liked turkey as a kid. |

DAVE. That stuff about growing up in an eighteen-room mansion?

JULIE. My sisters and I—every Thanksgiving—would fight for the dark meat ...

DAVE ... Not exactly true. It felt like it, being an only child and all ...

JULIE. ... and the wishbone. That's all I remember. "Who wants dark meat?" my father would say. "I do," I'd say. Then my little sister Molly—her voice an octave higher than normal— "May I have brown turkey, Daddy, please?" Suckered him every time. He'd cut so much, you know. Thanksgiving in our house lasted a week.

DAVE. My parents live in a three-bedroom Cape Cod.

JULIE. Cool.

DAVE. With a pool and ...

JULIE. ... a tennis court and gazebo in the backyard. See, I remember ...

DAVE. Well, actually in the park behind my house, well, beyond the alley and the street behind my house ...

JULIE. ... our second phone conversation. On time, just like you said. Honest, that was enough for me. I mean, to have a man actually call when he said he would and then to actually have a conversation ...

DAVE. I've said a lot of things ...

JULIE. We talked for two hours and I listened. I mean, no trying to be entertaining—trying to think of clever things to say. I just lay on the couch being soothed by the drone of your voice. I could have gone to sleep.

DAVE. I wish you had ...

JULIE. But I didn't.

DAVE. ... listened more closely ...

JULIE. That's how I knew you were the one for me. I mean the son of a housewife and a general practitioner ...

DAVE. Did I ever mention what my father practiced?

JULIE. ... who I now find out sacrificed the benefits of their sky-rocketing income to keep their son grounded in the real life, among real people ...

DAVE. Plumbing. Dad's a plumber. Mom runs a cleaning business.

JULIE. ... All this while sending him to our country's finest private school.

DAVE. A lot can be said for a public magnet school education ...

JULIE. ... Why? So that while you're developing your mind, you would be developing a sense of mission ...

DAVE. My mission ... my mission is you, it's us, it's ...

JULIE. Not that you would need a sense of mission after graduating from Purdue ...

DAVE. Did I say I graduated? I meant I attended—a seminar—on the solar system. I was twelve—eleven—and really into the planets, see ...

JULIE. I found your plans for revolutionizing the computer industry inspiring ...

DAVE. Well, yeah, computer programming. I can't do data entry forever.

JULIE. ... but not surprising, coming from you. You're a real self-made man, Dave. A real pioneer. All because your parents didn't overindulge you. I mean, giving you a Lexus, now, at age twenty-six ...

DAVE. You mean my grandfather's old Escort?

JULIE. And you never took it—until now.

DAVE. I can't—I couldn't ...

JULIE. I mean, really, Dave, you're being selfish. Sometimes, it's just as generous to receive as to give. Not that I mind renting the car for us this time ...

DAVE. I don't have a license. I never learned to drive.

JULIE. But think how much easier it will be getting around the city.

DAVE. Wait a minute. Is it me you like or the car I drive?

JULIE. Why you, of course, Dave. *(Pause.)* We're soul mates, don't you think? *(Pause.)* STATE LINE! Rest stop! I'm pulling over.

DAVE. You're mad. Look, I understand. I'll call my parents and explain everything.

JULIE. I'm not mad.

DAVE. I just wanted you to like me.

JULIE. Slide over.

*(JULIE gets out and runs around to DAVE's side of the car.)*

DAVE. What?

JULIE. Your turn to drive.

DAVE. But I couldn't. I can't.

JULIE. I bought the insurance.

DAVE. Haven't you heard anything ...?

JULIE. Driving and talking is one thing. But driving and listening ...

DAVE. I CAN NOT DRIVE!

JULIE. I heard you. *(Collects herself.)* Nerves, I guess. It's cold out here. I'm freezing.

*(JULIE starts pushing herself in on the passenger side.)*

DAVE. Julie, listen to me ...

JULIE. *(Angrily.)* MOVE!

*(DAVE hurriedly scoots over.)*

DAVE. *(Nervous.)* It's been so long since I ...

JULIE. The keys are in the ignition.

*(DAVE turns the key too far. The ignition screeches.)*

DAVE. Sorry.

JULIE. Everybody needs an extra push sometime, right? Me, the car, you ...

DAVE. You were always so encouraging. Nothing seemed impossible. *(JULIE stares straight ahead.)* D is for drive.

*(They jerk away.)*

 JULIE. Watch the speed bump.
 DAVE. I see it.
 JULIE. It means slow down. *(The car scrapes over the speed bump.)* Guess they didn't teach that at Purdue.
 DAVE. I just told you ...
 JULIE. Slow down and merge with the traffic. SLOW!

*(Sound of a car screeching by.)*

 DAVE. I can't do this.
 JULIE. Okay, go now. Go!

*(Sound of them speeding off.)*

 DAVE. You told me who you were ...
 JULIE. Not too fast ...
 DAVE. I told you who I wanted to be. *(Pause.)* Before you, there was no urgency.

*(Sound of truck beeping them from behind.)*

 JULIE. Not too slow either.
 DAVE. And then it seemed like so much ...
 JULIE. There's a truck on our tail.
 DAVE. I wanted desperately to please you ...
 JULIE. Speed up. Give him space to breathe.
 DAVE. Okay.
 JULIE. There.
 DAVE. Yeah. See, I can do this. And I can make it all up to ...
 JULIE. Pay attention! There's a detour ahead. What are you going to do?
 DAVE. I'll just move over.

*(DAVE turns the wheel to the right and is blasted by another vehicle.)*

 JULIE. You have to signal first. Make sure the coast is clear. And then move.
 DAVE. Okay.
 JULIE. Signal, look, move.
 DAVE. That's what I'm doing.
 JULIE. Slow down!

DAVE. SIGNAL, LOOK, MOVE!
JULIE. SLOW!

*(DAVE slams the brakes, bringing the car to a grinding halt.)*

DAVE. Are you okay?
JULIE. *(Shaken up.)* Always thinking about—thinking about me.
DAVE. Are you all right?
JULIE. I'm fine.
DAVE. The end ...
JULIE. Almost. If you hadn't stopped.

*(Pause.)*

DAVE. Look, I'll hitch a ride to my parents', you can go back to the city ...
JULIE. Each could have died never knowing who the other was.
DAVE. Listen, Julie ...
JULIE. Yes?
DAVE. Put the car in reverse, I'll direct you back on the road.
JULIE. You're going to stand behind a car driven by me?
DAVE. I trust you. Scoot over and wait for my signal. *(Gets out of the car. Yells from outside.)* Okay, come on.

*(Sound of wheels stuck and then releasing.)*

JULIE. I don't think it's working.
DAVE. A little more gas. You got it.
JULIE. I don't want to hurt you ...
DAVE. One more time ... Whew!
JULIE. Are you okay?
DAVE. Not a scratch. *(Comes around to her window.)* Well, I guess I'll be going. *(Pause.)* I used to worry about being overly morose, depressing, you know—crazy. I mean, who would want a suicidal, potentially homicidal boyfriend? But then I met you and...
JULIE. Want a ride?
DAVE. Really? Well, okay. Okay then. *(Runs around and jumps back in on the passenger side.)* My folks are simple, but they're pretty cool. We'll have a great time, I promise.
JULIE. I believe you.

**END OF PLAY**

# LAWYERS, GUNS, & MONEY

by

## Thad Davis

## LAWYERS, GUNS, & MONEY
### by Thad Davis

Directed by Lois Hall
Dramaturg: Amy Wegener

*Kevin:* C. Andrew Bauer
*Lydia:* Erica Blumfield
*Ford:* Matt Meyer

Scenic Designer: Tom Burch
Costume Designer: Renee Miller
Lighting Designers: Karen Hornberger, Matt Shuirr
Sound Designer: Jeremy Lee
Properties Designer: Craig Grigg
Stage Managers: John Armstrong, Catherine A. Kemp

### CHARACTERS
Ford, a man in his twenties.
Kevin, a man in his twenties.
Lydia, a woman in her twenties.

### SETTING
Kevin's apartment.

**A Note on the Gun:** A nine-millimeter automatic really would be best. Having said that, a revolver will do in a pinch. If the choice is made to go with a revolver please make the following changes:

Change Ford's "European Automatic." to ".357 Magnum." or ".38 Special." or whatever kind of gun is being used.

Change Kevin's "That nine-millimeter pistol you're holding ..." to "That six-shot revolver you're holding ..."

Finally, adjust all of the prices (Guesses, actual, wholesale, retail, etc.) downward by about a third.

## LAWYERS, GUNS, & MONEY

*(FORD, KEVIN and LYDIA, having drinks.)*

FORD. Lydia, leaving the program took courage.

KEVIN. ... to stare the Emperor in the eye and call him naked.

LYDIA. I'm frightened. I want to do good, but—

KEVIN. But? There's something else.

FORD. The ancients speak of glory.

LYDIA. Sometimes, I want to be like Ford.

FORD. Aha.

KEVIN. No. Not, "aha."

FORD. No, Lydia, I think you're on to something.

KEVIN. We all sometimes want to be like Ford. That's the point. His life, and the lives of those like him, are temptations, like cocaine, or being a gangster.

FORD. A gangster?

LYDIA. You want to be a gangster?

KEVIN. No, I don't want to be a gangster. But part of me does. A small part of me, finds it tempting.

LYDIA. Gangster, like a gang-banger or gangster, like the Mafia?

KEVIN. Like the Mafia. But my point is, when you examine the fantasy closely you see that it is not, in fact, something you would actually want. Like being a lawyer, like Ford.

LYDIA. I thought you wanted to be a Beastie Boy?

KEVIN. I do. That's not a temptation though, it's simply unrealistic. Given the chance, I would drop everything to be a Beastie Boy, with no moral qualms whatsoever.

FORD. Me too, I would drop everything if I could be a Beastie Boy.

LYDIA. Well maybe there's my answer.

KEVIN. I feel like you're mocking me now. Which is fine. But

35

I would hope that you would steer clear of my hopes and dreams
and confine your ridicule to what I do.

FORD. Which would be ... what?

LYDIA. Hope and dream?

KEVIN. There we go. That's more like it. Pretend that I don't
actually do anything worth talking about.

FORD. But Kevin, you don't. When we ask you what you've
been up to, you never talk about your job. It's not important to
you, why should it be important to us?

LYDIA. You're still doing temp work, right?

KEVIN. Yes.

FORD. Kevin, we take our cues from you.

LYDIA. Do you like it?

KEVIN. No. But it's very very easy.

FORD. Well okay then.

KEVIN. I'm going to show you something.

FORD. A new tattoo?

KEVIN. It will surprise you, and you might be a little upset.

LYDIA. I don't want to see it.

KEVIN. It's okay, it's nothing gross. It's ... well, a handgun.

*(KEVIN lays a gun on the table.)*

LYDIA. Oh, Kevin.

FORD. Kevin, it's okay. We love you—

KEVIN. Okay, this is what I was trying to avoid. Here, it's unloaded. Touch it.

LYDIA. I'm leaving.

FORD. Wait. Kevin, what's the matter? What's going on?

LYDIA. Kevin, I respect your temp work.

KEVIN. I'm going to stand up—

FORD. Oh, God—

KEVIN. —and step away from the gun. The gun will be by
itself, unloaded. And therefore it will not hurt us. *(KEVIN stands
up and steps away from the gun.)* Let's all breathe. *(They breathe.)*
Ford, Lydia, I have a business proposition.

LYDIA. You *are* a gangster.

FORD. A heist. You're planning a heist and you're letting us in.
Damn.

KEVIN. No heist. What I'm proposing is completely legal. In
fact, if anything seems otherwise, *Ford*, I'd like you to tell me.

LYDIA. You are shrewd.

FORD. Already planning your defense. Attorney client privi-
lege.

KEVIN. How much do you think this cost?

FORD. Is it hot?

LYDIA. Two hundred dollars.

KEVIN. No, I purchased it legally, retail. There was a waiting period, and I have a permit.

LYDIA. Three hundred.

KEVIN. Ford?

FORD. Let me see it.

*(FORD picks up the gun.)*

LYDIA. Ford!

KEVIN. It's okay. What do you think?

FORD. European automatic. I'm assuming it's not counterfeit. Twelve hundred.

KEVIN. I paid eight hundred dollars for this.

FORD. What are you going to do with it?

LYDIA. Ford, put it down.

KEVIN. Let Lydia hold it.

LYDIA. No!

KEVIN. C'mon, give it a try.

FORD. C'mon, Lydia.

LYDIA. Why, what for?

KEVIN. Because you can. Because it's your right. Like voting, or freely practicing your religion.

LYDIA. I think the Second Amendment is suspect as written, and even more so as interpreted. I favor strict gun laws.

KEVIN. So do I, Lydia.

FORD. Don't we all?

LYDIA. Are you proposing we form a well-regulated militia?

KEVIN. Take the gun, Lydia. It's not loaded.

LYDIA. That's the oldest mistake in the book.

KEVIN. That's just the kind of smart, responsible thinking that makes me comfortable giving you a gun.

FORD. It's pretty nice, Lydia. It's surprisingly heavy.

KEVIN. Take it. Handle it as if it were loaded.

*(LYDIA takes the gun.)*

FORD. There we go.

KEVIN. It looks good, Lydia. How does it feel?

LYDIA. Okay. It has heft. It's like a machine.

KEVIN. What do you think that cost wholesale?

LYDIA. I don't know about things like that. Seven hundred?

FORD. Three, four hundred.

KEVIN. This weapon wholesales for about five hundred dollars.

FORD. You're going to sell them to gangsters from the trunk of your car. There's a shipment waiting at the border. Am I right?

LYDIA. Kevin, that's bad.

FORD. Nasty.

LYDIA. What would happen if I pulled the trigger?

FORD. Don't.

KEVIN. Well, remember we're operating on the new assumption that this gun *is* loaded. But even if it weren't, it's not a good idea to pull the trigger. It's "bad" for the gun.

LYDIA. Like an empty coffee pot on a hot burner?

FORD. That's an excellent analogy.

KEVIN. Yes, not the end of the world, but neither is it a good idea. Ford, there will be no selling of guns to gangsters. And the whole "trunk of my car" bit seems a little sordid. But, I am proposing that we get into the gun business.

LYDIA. Like open a store?

KEVIN. Are you guys familiar with the term "multi-level distribution"?

FORD. Oh, Kevin.

KEVIN. Your reaction is completely understandable.

LYDIA. What's "multi-level distribution"?

FORD. Try "pyramid scheme."

KEVIN. Technically, "pyramid schemes" are illegal. Now—

LYDIA. What, is this like, what's the name of that company—

KEVIN. Don't say it.

LYDIA. My cousin tricked me into going to a meeting, then I had to buy a bunch of soap and bad gum.

FORD. You set us up. This whole get-together-for-drinks was all a set-up so that you could get us into your cult. You're going to bring in some guy who'll "let us in on an opportunity."

KEVIN. There's no cult.

FORD. Some sort of pyramid gun cult.

LYDIA. I feel dirty. You made me hold the gun. That's a trick they tell you to do.

KEVIN. There's no they. This is me. My idea. Yes, there's a pyramid, or there will be, but it's ours. We're at the top.

FORD. Selling guns?

KEVIN. Yes. To our friends. And at the same time encouraging them to do likewise. We make money from what we sell, and more importantly, we get a cut from what they sell, and so on and so on. Exponentially. Like a pyramid.

LYDIA. Because of multiplication.

KEVIN. Yes.

FORD. We don't exactly hang with the gun crowd, Kevin.

KEVIN. That's the point. The people we know wouldn't dream of walking into a gun store. But most of them, if given a chance, privately, would be thrilled to handle a firearm. And would be surprised to know that they could afford one.

LYDIA. Guns are inherently dangerous.

FORD. The world's inherently dangerous.

LYDIA. Statistically a gun is more likely to be used against its owner than in actual defense of the owner.

KEVIN. Statistically, a person is more likely to believe in alien abductions than they are to vote. I trust myself and my judgment, and I'm counting on my friends to do likewise.

FORD. Would you sell to Jake?

KEVIN. Jake Ingram? Sure.

FORD. But what about his wife?

KEVIN. What about her?

LYDIA. She's heavily medicated. And she breaks things in anger.

KEVIN. Right. I would caution Jake to consider his domestic situation, as I would anyone, particularly households with children. I would encourage him to purchase a trigger lock and lockbox, but ultimately the decision would be his.

FORD. It could be complicated, legally.

KEVIN. Dealer permits are cheap and easy to get. And there's a conceal and carry bill before the legislature that if passed—

FORD. —could blow this thing wide open, right. But I'm a little concerned about the lack of potential for repeat business.

KEVIN. Don't be. Once you buy one, you'll find yourself wanting more. This is my third. Talk to me, Lydia.

LYDIA. I feel ashamed.

FORD. Shame's unhealthy. That's your momma talking.

LYDIA. My mother is righteous, enlightened and liberated. This would break her heart.

KEVIN. Lydia, I respect your mother. I respect the work she's done. ERA, pro-choice, child-care, all of that has been about options and self-determination for women. That nine-millimeter pistol you're holding, that's just another step. That's just another set of options that traditionally women have been denied, but which are legally and morally theirs by right. Your mother wasn't afraid to shock her mother. And she didn't raise you to be afraid to shock her.

*(Pause.)*

LYDIA. I could sell her one.

KEVIN. Give it to her as a gift, with lessons.

LYDIA. Sometimes nasty is good.

FORD. So, is this a scam or a legitimate business?

KEVIN. We're at the top of the pyramid, I don't think it has to be either/or. We're selling a quality product, aggressively.

LYDIA. What are we selling? Guns?

FORD. Security.

LYDIA. Or the pyramid?

KEVIN. Opportunity.

LYDIA. Power.

FORD. Power.

KEVIN. Without that, you can't really be said to have it all, now can you?

FORD. Lydia.

LYDIA. Yes, Ford?

FORD. Are you still afraid?

LYDIA. No. Not at all.

*(LYDIA pulls the trigger, the gun goes off. Pause. Everyone bursts into laughter.)*

FORD. Yeah.

KEVIN. I'm going to get me a big-ass Suburban—dark green, bulletproof.

**END OF PLAY**

# ACORN

by

**David Graziano**

## ACORN
### by David Graziano

Directed by Sandra Grand
Dramaturg: Sarah Achbach

*Bags:* Matthew Damico
*Catherine:* Catherine Papafotis

Scenic Designer: Tom Burch
Costume Designer: Katherine Hampton
Lighting Designer: Greg Sullivan
Sound Designer: Jason A. Tratta
Properties Designer: Mark Walston
Stage Managers: Heather Fields, Juliet Horn,
Charles M. Turner III

# ACORN

*(Darkness. Lights come up on a male and a female. The male is Vincent "Bags" Baggaruso. He is a 26-year-old unemployed union carpenter. The female is Catherine Dinoffrio, she is an 18-year-old just out of high school who takes care of her invalid father. There is a clothesline with a pulley extending from Bags to Catherine.)*

CATHERINE. Vincent Baggaruso? ... "Bags"?

BAGS. Catherine Dinoffrio? *(Savoring her name.)* Catherine Dinoffrio ...

CATHERINE. He disgusts me ...

BAGS. It was weird. I mean I'm on this union job, you know, carpentry—a product launch for this new kinda beeper ... see I even got one. Anyway, at a certain point in the show they wanted these doves to fly out over the crowd. I told them I could build a box that could be flipped over at the right time ... you know to let the birds loose ...

CATHERINE. I felt trapped. Here I am, just out of high school, wanting to go away to college like the rest of the neighborhood and ... my father got sick ... *(Whispering.)* Colon cancer. What was I to do? Leave him to some Haitian nurse? Uh-uh, we're family.

BAGS. I loved jobs like this. I mean cake—pure cake. So, I made sure that box was built, you know, good. *(Laughing.)* Well I wound up makin' the box so good that it was almost airtight. By the time they flipped the box over all but two of the doves had died.

CATHERINE. I felt bad though. Restless. Like all boxed in. I felt guilty, like I was waitin' for my father to ... die.

BAGS. So the doves fall out and ... wham ... land on top of some people from Indianapolis. You think they'd stop the show? Uh-uh. Anyway, I got fired an' that's how I wound up at my uncle's place and ... ohhh ... Catherine ...

CATHERINE. Sunday I do the rugs. Vacuum and shampoo. Wednesday I make sure my father gets to see the doctor. And every day I do laundry. I got two little brothers and I'll be damned if they look like slobs. Wha, my mother? She cut out as soon as pop was diagnosed 'cause when he was healthy he used to beat—

*(CATHERINE catches herself.)*

BAGS. Well my uncle don't allow no smokin' in his house. Good thing too, 'cause I had to go out onto the patio. Well one day I was on that patio thinkin' about how I'm almost 26 an' I'm outta work. An' then I look up an' see these little underwears, like from a girl—er, a woman rather.

CATHERINE. I noticed Bags looking at me the second day he moved in. I know his uncle next door a long time ...

BAGS. You ever notice on girls', I mean, women's underwear how they got those little ribbons in the shape of a bow? Shit. That's cute. The guy that invented that? He's some kinda genius ... you know, my mind started goin' an', before I knew it ...

CATHERINE. Before I knew it he was staring at me every day as I put the laundry out. Ten o'clock came and he'd be out there smokin' his cigarette.

BAGS. Don't get the wrong idea. I ain't a freak. I mean I never dress in girls' underwear or nothing.

CATHERINE. Something wasn't right about him. He seemed, I don't know ... retarded ...

BAGS. My grandfather always said, when a Baggarusso falls in love—he falls! I stared at those underwears so long sometimes, that the sun would hurt my eyes. At least twenty feet high they were, from her window to the telephone pole. Well, one time I looked down 'cause of the sun an' there were these acorns all over the cement ... so I threw some ... as a joke. At the window first ... and then ...

CATHERINE. I was taking in the laundry and all these acorns were in the clothes—my panties especially—in clean clothes!? Uh-uh. I rewashed everything. Who knows where those acorns were.

BAGS. It just seemed to fit. I mean ... acorns ... panties. Besides I couldn't touch 'em, they were up too high. I figured for a joke ... I could touch somethin' that would touch her underwear ... which in turn would touch her. If that's the closest I could come to her, I would be happy. Hey, I'm not a freak ... just for fun ... you know ...

CATHERINE. Doing that extra load that day made me sooo mad! You know what I did? I took all those acorns and laid them out on his uncle's welcome mat in the shape of what I thought Bags was ... an ass!

BAGS. When she gave the acorns back, I knew it was a symbol. She arranged them in the shape of a heart.

CATHERINE. I figured he would get the hint. But after the ass-shaped acorns, he started leaving notes. Pinning them ... in the night ... to my underwear ... on the line!

BAGS. I stayed up all night writing the note. And I got a ladder from the garage. I rolled the note up real tight and thin and slipped it in the little pink bow on the front of the underwear ...

CATHERINE. I had to end this before my brothers or my father found out. I mean, what if the neighbors saw!?

BAGS. This, now this, was the beginning to somethin' really special.

CATHERINE. So ... I started wearing guys' underwear. I went right out after he put the second note in my panties and bought some briefs, nice colored ones. Couldn't find pink though.

BAGS. On the third night I'm puttin' another note—that makes three now—and I gotta lean off of the ladder a little bit ... big ladder ... old ... rickety ... you know sort of into her yard ... 'cause there's this fence between us ...

CATHERINE. You'd be surprised how much more comfortable guys' underwear is than girls'. No wedgies, no nothin'. *(Laughing.)* And that little flap ...

BAGS. Well I rolled it up real tight and slipped it in, this note was a little longer so it was harder to get it in the bow on her underwears, and ... "bam!" I lost my balance! The ... the ladder kicked out from beneath me and *(Makes hitting sound.)* my leg was broke. I knew it right off the bat. I heard the crack an' everything.

CATHERINE. I got two little brothers and I didn't know what that flap was for! *(Laughing.)* Of course I have no use for it. But it's sooo cute ... you don't think I'm a freak, right?

BAGS. Would you know I climbed back over the fence and put the ladder away and everything—all with a broken leg! And I knew my grandfather was laughin 'cause I could hear him say, "When a Baggarusso falls in love ... he falls."

*(BAGS is laughing.)*

CATHERINE. Well it worked, the guys' underwear, I wore some every day. I'm even wearing some right now. *(Shows the band.)* He actually stopped writing notes.

BAGS. Needless to say I couldn't leave her notes anymore, at least not for awhile. Man that thing took forever to heal ... and itchy!?

CATHERINE. It was nice but it was a strange sort of silence ... and I went back to taking care of my father ...

BAGS. I convinced my uncle to switch rooms with me 'cause I told him that his room was closer to the bathroom. Well, my uncle's room has this great view ... of her washline. At least I could see what she wore that day, right? You know, open my window an' maybe smell her detergent ... anything ...

CATHERINE. I started thinking about what he thought about...

BAGS. I dunno. I mean there were no panties, so I waited. I started thinkin', maybe she didn't wear any that day, you know, the kinky type.

CATHERINE. His letters *were* kind of romantic, I mean, for a guy who writes with a Brooklyn accent.

BAGS. Well after a week I got pissed. What!? She didn't wear panties for a whole week!? What else? I mean what's she got under her bed? Whips? Hot candle wax? Black mambos?

CATHERINE. I'd like to marry a guy who's romantic, like the "boy next door" type.

BAGS. Uh-uh, I'm sorry. This ain't the type of girl a guy wants to marry. And that guys' underwear out there, it's too big for her brothers. An' her father wears boxers. I know. I been watchin' ...

CATHERINE. I cooked and cleaned and vacuumed and flipped channels and shaved my father, but the laundry. I realized laundry for what it was. It's not just another household chore ... it's a form of communication ...

BAGS. I broke my leg for this? Forget it. I stopped waiting. I don't care if all the clotheslines in all the neighborhoods in the world were full of panties, floral printed, frilly panties, with bows, French cut an' all, who cares!

CATHERINE. Being cooped up in that house like a pigeon, who needs it, I began to miss the notes ... more and more and more...

BAGS. I didn't care about women. Forgettaboutem! Not real ones at least. I got my uncle to get me couple of old *Cosmos* from the dental office where he works.

CATHERINE. I felt stifled ... suffocated ...

BAGS. I read up on what women really liked for weeks. I took twenty-three romance quizzes, memorized all of the supermodels' names and learned a little bit more than I needed to know about toxic shock syndrome.

CATHERINE. I was lonely.

BAGS. There's no denyin' it ... I was horny.

CATHERINE. I couldn't take it ... being so isolated. I just needed a friend. So, just for kicks, I put one pair of panties up on the clothesline—nothing sexy, just pink, with a little ribbon shaped like a bow.

BAGS. Oh my god!

CATHERINE. I waited and decided to leave those panties up there all night long ...

BAGS. Oh my god!

CATHERINE. I woke up the next morning ... and nothing. Can guys really be that fickle? I mean one minute they're putting notes in your panties and then nothing. Just because a girl plays hard to get.

BAGS. I couldn't do nothin'! I tried gettin' the phone number from my uncle, "The father is on his deathbed and you're gonna be messin' with his daughter?" I told him it was alright. I told him about the reappearance of the panties an' everything. I told him how it was a symbol. I even told him the real way that I broke my leg. He looked at me like I had a hole in my head.

CATHERINE. So, I saw, he wanted to play hard to get with me now. Uh-uh. Catherine Dinoffrio is no man's violin. She will not be played.

BAGS. Oh my god!!

CATHERINE. Yep! Every color, size, shape imaginable, they all went up. I even took a trip to Victoria's Secret and bought some new French cuts, a thong and several silk slips. I read somewhere that silk slips drive men nuts. *Cosmo* I think. I left the panties up overnight.

BAGS. That night I learned how to go down the stairs on my ass. I got out in that patio ... looked at all those panties blowing in the moonlight ... wit' all those bows ... and had my first cigarette in what seemed like months. I picked a single acorn from the ground ... I threw it just right ... real gentle against the glass ... and she came to her window ... that night ... at her window ... Catherine spoke the first words she would ever speak to me. It was the first time I would ever hear her voice ... she said ...

CATHERINE. You're a freak!

BAGS. And it's true. Maybe I am.

CATHERINE. We went on our first date two nights after that ... and three months from then my father passed away.

BAGS. Yeah, an' four days after that, my uncle threw me out. But now me an' Catherine share our own clothesline.

CATHERINE. Just you, me ... an' my brothers.

BAGS. Now that's romance ... that's romance.

*(They kiss.*
*Blackout.)*

**END OF PLAY**

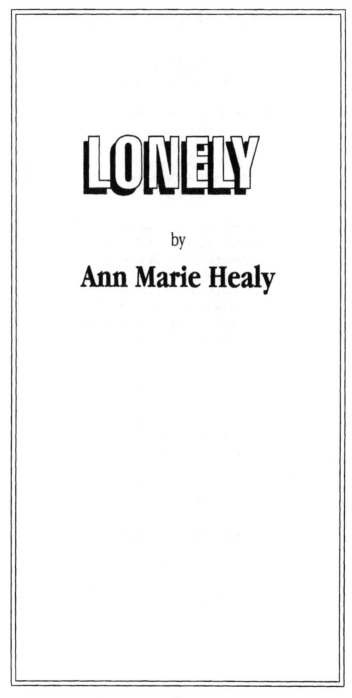

# LONELY

by

## Ann Marie Healy

## LONELY
### by Ann Marie Healy

Directed by Michael Bigelow Dixon
Dramaturg: Megan Shultz

*Milly:* Hilary Redmon
*Frank:* Shawn Fagan
*Frances:* Sara Sommervold

Scenic Designer: Tom Burch
Costume Designer: Emily McConnell
Lighting Designer: Paul Werner
Sound Designer: Jason A. Tratta
Properties Designer: Mark Walston
Stage Manager: Jennifer Wills
Assistant Stage Managers: Patty Thoreson,
Laura Jean Wickman

## CHARACTERS

Frank—late twenties
Milly—late twenties
Frances—Milly's sister, early twenties

## SETTING

Frank and Milly's house

## LONELY

*(FRANK, MILLY and FRANCES enter the living room.)*

MILLY. And this is the living room. This is where we do the living.

FRANK. The living. Right. A man needs to live. In a room.

FRANCES. It's great.

MILLY. It is great.

FRANK. This is a great place to sit and think. Sometimes I come in here and think to myself.

MILLY. Or you think out loud.

FRANK. True. I might think out loud. If Milly's in here, I think out loud and she listens. *(To himself.)* I think that I used to be scared of the winter. *(To MILLY and FRANCES.)* You see, I'm thinking out loud right now.

MILLY. *(To FRANCES.)* It's so dark—the winter, that's what he means. *(To FRANK.)* Is that what you mean?

FRANK. Sort of. More cold than dark. You were close.

FRANCES. At least it's warm inside your house.

MILLY. Right. Frank sits there and I sit here and we get a big stack of wood from outside and make a fire.

FRANK. Cozy. It's very cozy. That's living.

MILLY. I make Hot Toddies sometimes. We never let it get cold like Mom and Dad's. Mom would never serve a Hot Toddy.

FRANK. Homebodies. That's how I've always liked to fancy myself. *(FRANK grabs MILLY and kisses her.)* I'll tell you though, it's a lot a more fun being a homebody when there's another body there.

MILLY. I'm the body! I'm the body!

FRANK. She's the body. I'm the brains.

FRANCES. Right, right.

FRANK. That was my joke.

MILLY. No. He's the brawn. He's the muscle that turns the corks. Or the screws. Or ... how does that saying go?

FRANCES. What saying?

MILLY. The saying about making the machinery go?

FRANK. Oh ... right. Right. She means I make the machinery go. *(Pause.)* Are you talking about my toolshop?

MILLY. Well ... yes. But also in a larger sense.

FRANCES. Milly is always thinking in a larger sense.

MILLY. Why do you say that?

FRANCES. Your mind never rests on the situation at hand.

MILLY. That's not true.

FRANK. What is the larger sense of my toolshop?

MILLY. There is no larger sense Frank.

FRANK. Right, right. Have you been downstairs Frances?

FRANCES. Not yet.

MILLY. The other day Frank spent the entire morning—well you tell it. I can't tell it.

FRANK. The other day I what?

MILLY. You spent the day in the basement and ... You tell the story. I can't tell stories.

FRANK. Oh ... we don't need to tell that story.

MILLY. But it's funny.

FRANK. *(Holds up hand to reveal bandage around his finger.)* The ending is no fun. It wasn't really that funny.

MILLY. *(Pause.)* Right. The ending is no fun. *(To FRANCES.)* It was funny at the time though.

FRANCES. I'm sure. I can sort of imagine it.

MILLY. You can?

FRANCES. I mean the part about the basement.

MILLY. Good.

FRANCES. I can imagine it being very funny.

*(Pause.)*

MILLY. Frank, put on some music will you?

FRANK. Something fast? Something slow?

MILLY. Frank likes bongos.

FRANK. Likes? Loves.

FRANCES. Something slow.

*(FRANK exits. Music plays softly. MILLY and FRANCES stand in silence.)*

MILLY. You're not happy.

FRANCES. Sure I am.

MILLY. What's wrong?

FRANCES. Nothing's wrong.

MILLY. Are you lonely?

FRANCES. No.

MILLY. I thought you might be lonely.

FRANCES. Not very.

MILLY. Well if you are ... don't be.

FRANCES. All right.

MILLY. Now you're being sarcastic.

FRANCES. I'm not.

MILLY. You know what it is don't you?

FRANCES. What what is?

MILLY. The reason.

FRANCES. No.

MILLY. *(Whispering.)* Mom and Dad are getting older.

FRANCES. So are you.

MILLY. Well so are you. You'll have to leave home sometime.

FRANCES. I like it there.

MILLY. That's what I thought too. Then I left. And now *(She motions around the room.)* I have this. *(Pause.)* Do you know Frank and I put a couch in our bedroom? I've always wanted to put a couch in my bedroom and he said to just do it and now when I walk into the bedroom he says "Hey you! Come sit on the bed." And then I walk over and sit on the couch. You know why? Because they're both in my bedroom.

FRANCES. I have my bedroom the way I like it. There's not much clutter. *(Pause.)* People are clutter.

MILLY. Only the wrong person is clutter. The right person is the treat at the end of the long maze. The reward for being lost! Maybe you're lost, Frances?

*(Pause.)*

FRANCES. I have been talking to myself lately.

MILLY. You always talk to yourself.

FRANCES. But lately, I've been ... responding to myself in a different voice.

MILLY. What kind of voice?

FRANCES. *(Pause.)* There are a few ... different voices. Some are ... rowdier than others.

MILLY. Frances.

FRANCES. What?

MILLY. You're lonely.

FRANCES. So?

MILLY. What ever happened to Bill?

FRANCES. Bob?

MILLY. Bob.

FRANCES. Nothing.

MILLY. Why?

FRANCES. *(Pause.)* I made him up.

MILLY. What?

FRANCES. And Chuck and Mo and Phillip ...

MILLY. All of them?

FRANCES. Yes.

MILLY. But they weren't even nice to you. Didn't Mo cheat on you?

FRANCES. Twice ... Once with Phillip.

MILLY. Why did you lie?

FRANCES. So I would have something to talk about ... with you.

MILLY. We have things to talk about Frances ... Don't we?

FRANCES. I don't know.

*(Pause.)*

MILLY. What did you do all those nights?

FRANCES. I went to the movies. I went to diners. I walked around ... I did things. That's what I'm trying to tell you, Milly. I have a lot of fun.

MILLY. What kind of fun?

FRANCES. I just told you.

MILLY. Oh. *(Pause.)* Well it's not the worst thing.

FRANCES. What?

MILLY. Being lonely.

FRANCES. I know.

MILLY. No you don't. It's not the worst thing because it makes everything better in the end.

FRANCES. What end?

MILLY. The end of the maze. That thing that you find when you're lonely.

FRANCES. Thing?

MILLY. Frank.

FRANCES. *(Pause.)* Oh.

*(FRANK returns from the other room.)*

FRANK. There's a particular bongo that plays in the background of this song. Shhh ... Everybody listen.

*(They stop for a moment to listen.)*

FRANCES. I don't hear it.

FRANK. Neither do I. That's funny ... I'm sure it's there.

MILLY. Your hearing is going. In your old age.

FRANK. My old age ... I was calculating my years last night, and I spent the majority of my life unhappy. *(FRANK turns to FRANCES.)* Do you know I spent the majority of my life unhappy?

MILLY. Frances is unhappy right now.

FRANK. Are you?

FRANCES. I never said that.

MILLY. She's lonely.

FRANK. Frances ... Are you lonely? I was lonely too. Really. *(Pause. )* I would say seven-eighths of my life I was lonely because for that amount of time, divided up mathematically, I was without your sister.

FRANCES. I know. You did the math in your marriage proposal.

FRANK. My proposal. Frances, how do you think I fancied myself that day?

FRANCES. I remember your suit.

FRANK. I fancied myself a sort of ambassador. Me, inviting all of you into my world. That's why I wore a suit. Ambassadors need to make a good impression.

FRANCES. But you're not wearing a suit right now.

FRANK. I'm not. But that was the day I decided to dress up my thoughts too. Even if I'm not wearing a suit, my brain is always wearing a tuxedo. Do you see?

FRANCES. The tuxedo?

FRANK. No. Not just the tuxedo. *(Pause.)* Look at Milly. Milly's got to primp her brain too. Like if she's got an evening gown on her mind *(FRANK takes a moment to visualize this.)*, we can imagine the courtship of our two thoughts.

MILLY. The end of the maze.

FRANK. Like those little rodents that sneak their heads out of the ground and look around. *(To FRANCES.)* That's how I felt before I met your sister. There was always dirt in my eyes.

MILLY. Exactly. That's what I'm saying, Frances.

FRANK. The problem is, you're looking at the world as if there was some answer.

FRANCES. I'm not looking for answers.

MILLY. There's nothing wrong with looking for answers.

FRANCES. Actually I'm not. Really. I might have been before but I'm here now and I think I understand and I'm not.

FRANK. But you're looking for something so look at the two of us as an example. I spent my entire life looking for something and when I realized it didn't exist I was a much happier person.

MILLY. *(Pause.)* Thanks.

FRANK. No, thank you honey.

FRANCES. *(To MILLY.)* We shouldn't talk about this anymore.

FRANK. But we haven't gotten to the beauty, the beauty of giving over. You just accept that no one is you. You see? And once you do that, you can accept that no one is right for you. And then, then you can finally settle down into the living. *(Looking around the living room.)* Settling into this room for example ... Settling in all ways. *(Pause.)* I could go for a Hot Toddy right now. Milly? *(Pause.)* All right. *(FRANK goes to make a drink. The three sit in silence. FRANK mumbles.)* Put on the tuxedo Frank! Time to put on that tuxedo. *(To MILLY.)* Thinking out loud again. Milly, you caught me thinking out loud again.

FRANCES. Thinking what?

FRANK. Just thinking that you shouldn't worry about it, Frances.

FRANCES. Right.

FRANK. Right, Milly?

MILLY. *(Staring at FRANK.)* Right, Frank.

*(MILLY gets up and exits. FRANK looks at the door, waiting for MILLY's return. A long pause.)*

**FRANK. Right.**

*(FRANCES and FRANK sit silent in the living room. The lights fade.)*

**END OF PLAY**

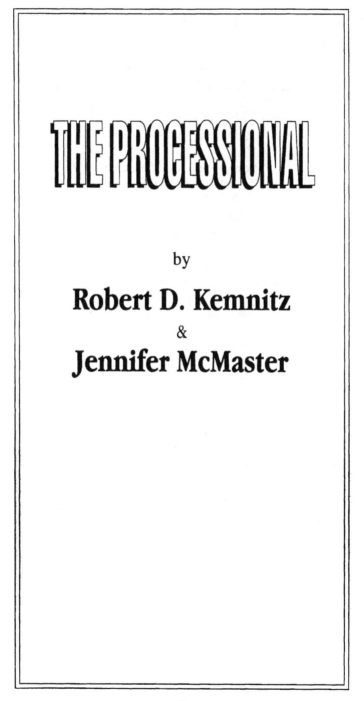

# THE PROCESSIONAL

by

## Robert D. Kemnitz

&

## Jennifer McMaster

## THE PROCESSIONAL
### by Robert D. Kemnitz and Jennifer McMaster

Directed by Stuart Carden
Dramaturg: Sarah Achbach

*Pastor*: Arthur Allen Doederlein
*Dillon:* Eric Bryant
*Fay:* Woodwyn Koons
*Jarod:* Geoffrey Hillback
*Jackie:* Hilary Redmon

Scenic Designer: Tom Burch
Costume Designer: Emily McConnell
Lighting Designer: Paul Werner
Sound Designer: Mark Huang
Properties Designer: Mark Walston
Stage Manager: Jennifer Wills
Assistant Stage Managers: Patty Thoreson, Laura Jean Wickman

# THE PROCESSIONAL

(*A small [black box] church. There are two podiums on either side of the stage. For the altar, two or three padded steps for kneeling.*
*At rise, the PASTOR and DILLON stand by the altar.*)

PASTOR. Okay, I know we're all a little tired. But... Once more with feeling. (*JAROD, the Best Man, escorts JACKIE, Maid of Honor, towards the altar.*) Good, good. It's not a funeral, we can put a little pizazz into it. (*JAROD and JACKIE part in front of the PASTOR and go to their respective sides.*) And of course tomorrow we will be in step together. Now the Father of the Bride takes the Bride-to-Be by the arm to lead the procession. (*DILLON tries to conceal a yawn. To DILLON.*) I'm sorry, are we boring you? (*FAY enters, trying to step to unheard music. She carries with her the bouquet of wilted bows and ribbons from last weekend's shower.*) Lovely, lovely—where's the Father of the Bride?

DILLON. He left.

PASTOR. Oh?

DILLON. About thirty minutes ago. He left after the fifth reprise of "O Promise Me."

FAY. He said we could meet him and Mother at the restaurant.

PASTOR. Well, apparently he's not as concerned with his daughter's wedding as I am. I guess he'll just have to wing it. Generally, I don't approve of improvisational weddings. I certainly hope your father doesn't spoil the whole ceremony because he had better things to do the night of the rehearsal. A wedding day is not a day for surprises. (*To FAY.*) You wouldn't want that. On your wedding day.

FAY. Actually, we are looking forward to some surprises.

*(FAY giggles. DILLON beams.)*

JACKIE. Fay!

PASTOR. Oh, expecting the big screen TV, are we?

FAY. Something like that.

JAROD. Do we know how much longer ... ?

PASTOR. I see everyone's got big plans for the evening—I'm sorry to hold you up. But as I explained in my one, brief meeting with Dillon and Fay, I like things to be done right, and I like things to be done my way, and my way is the right way. Of course, we didn't have much time to go over the details, since we only met once, briefly, last week, Tuesday was it?—After I hadn't seen Fay since her confirmation when she was fourteen years old and Dillon, upon whom I had never laid eyes prior to our one, brief meeting. For all I know he's a Catholic.

DILLON. Lutheran.

PASTOR. Whatever. Let's get on with it, shall we. *(Everyone relaxes.)* My critique of the opening pageant is charitable at best. The entrances set the whole tone for the ceremony, and right now I'm greatly concerned—the rhythm is off and the gait is, well, downright downtrodden. *(Quiet grumbles.)* But in the interest of time, we won't go back. I will say a few remarks, dearly beloved, please be seated, that sort of thing, and now, the first scripture reading. I believe the Best Man will be doing the honors.

JAROD. Yes... sir.

PASTOR. Well then?

JAROD. Well—I've been practicing, I think it'll be fine. I don't think we need to hold up things for me.

PASTOR. Oh, you don't, do you? I for one would like to hear it this time 'round. Those Bible passages can be tricky for plebeians. *(JAROD hesitates.)* Today, son!

*(JAROD sprints to the podium. He extracts a crumpled piece of paper from his pocket.)*

JAROD. The first reading today is from I, Corinthians—

*(JAROD pronounces it "aye".)*

PASTOR. That's First Corinthians.

JAROD. First Corinthians, yes, right, Chapter 7, Verse 1: *(Boldly, and gaining boldness.)* "It is well for a man not to touch a woman. But because of the temptation to immorality, each man should have his own wife and each woman her own husband. The husband should give to his wife her conjugal rights, and likewise the wife to her husband. For the wife does not rule over her own body, but the husband does; likewise the husband does not rule over his own body, but the wife does. Do not refuse one another except perhaps by agreement for a season, that you may devote yourselves to prayer; but then come together again, lest Satan tempt you through lack of self-control. To the unmarried and the widows I say that it is well for them to remain single as I do. But if they cannot exercise self-control, they should marry. For it is better to marry than to be aflame with passion."

FAY and DILLON. Amen.

PASTOR. *(Long pause.)* That's... the passage you chose for your first scripture reading?

FAY. Yes. Isn't it romantic?

DILLON. Well done, Jarod.

PASTOR. Bombastic, to say the least. Did you, by any chance, listen to the words?

DILLON. Of course.

FAY. I know it by heart.

PASTOR. And this is the first scripture you chose to begin your new life as man and wife?

DILLON. Husband and wife.

PASTOR. You're prepared for your family and friends to hear these words as a testament to your life together?

FAY. Not just hear it—we've had it printed on the reception napkins. "For it is better to marry..."

DILLON. It is right out of the Bible.

PASTOR. Ah, yes. "Aye" Corinthians, as we've just discovered. What I mean is, it's very... "Old Testament"—do you know? Today, in modern times, we are allowed to interpret the Word of the Lord—

DILLON. No room for interpretation there.

FAY. It says everything we want to say, just how we would say it.

JAROD. *(From podium.)* Can I come down now?

PASTOR. Yes, perhaps you should. Before we invoke the seven plagues. *(JAROD moves back to his position. The pastor takes a moment.)* Well, I'll have to come up with something to follow that. Maybe I can address it in my sermon.

DILLON. I hate to rush you, but we do have quite a few people waiting for us at the dinner.

PASTOR. Of course, wouldn't want your guests to hog all the stuffed mushrooms, now would we. The church can wait, the rumaki cannot!

DILLON. It's not that I don't appreciate—

PASTOR. No, no, you're quite right. I think that we should move on to the second reading, and yes, I'd love to hear it. I think that's you, Matron of Honor.

JACKIE. Maid of Honor.

PASTOR. I was under the understanding that you were the Matron of Honor.

JACKIE. I was. Until last week. Now I'm the Maid of Honor.

PASTOR. Oh.

JACKIE. It happened pretty quick. Actually, it had been going on for years. First I found out—

PASTOR. *(Changing the subject.)* Which brings up the Maid of Honor with the second scripture reading.

*(JACKIE moves up to the other pulpit, a deer caught in the headlights.)*

JACKIE. *(Meekly.)* The second reading is from Ezekiel, Chapter 16, Verse 30. *(She gently clears her throat. Bellowing:)* "Wherefore, O harlot, hear the word of the Lord! Because your shame was laid bare and your nakedness uncovered in your harlotries with your lovers... Therefore, behold, I will gather all your lovers, with whom you took pleasure, all those you loved and all those you loathed. And I will judge you as women who break wedlock and shed blood are judged, and bring upon you the blood of wrath and jealousy. And I will give you into the hand of your lovers, and they shall throw down your vaulted chamber and break down your lofty places; they shall strip you of your clothes and take your fair jewels, and leave you naked and bare. They shall bring up a host against you, and they shall stone you and cut you to pieces with their swords—

PASTOR. Stop! Stop! You're melting the pulpit!

JACKIE. Did I do something wrong?

PASTOR. Are you packing snakes?

DILLON. She's just a little tired.

PASTOR. Now, I like to think I know Ezekiel, he's an inspiration to us all—but this? Why in God's name did you choose this?

FAY. Because it expresses our feelings about sin and immorality and jealousy and shame and sex out of wedlock.

DILLON. It couldn't be any clearer.

PASTOR. No, it sure couldn't. The blood and wrath of jealousy I'm all for, but your nakedness uncovered in your harlotries... ? Wait. You two haven't done the nasty.

DILLON. Your use of the term nasty speaks volumes.

PASTOR. Actually it speaks Genesis to Revelation. Had we had more meetings, maybe we could have covered this. I, of course, just assumed you two had been familiar with one another.

FAY. We're very familiar with one another.

DILLON. She clips her toenails in the bathroom sink.

FAY. He eats M&Ms for breakfast.

PASTOR. I meant familiar in the Biblical sense. I've had a feeling all along about this wedding—something wrong. I knew it, but I couldn't quite put my finger on it. This nagging doubt...

FAY. That's why we've been stuck here for two and a half hours? You've held us hostage all this time because something didn't sit right with you?

PASTOR. Frankly. Yes.

DILLON. You have no right to do that. It's your job to marry us!

PASTOR. This is not McDonald's. I don't have a sign over my sacristy reading, "Two billion served." And you will not get fries with this.

JAROD. Can we not talk about food right now? I'm starving.

PASTOR. I'm just worried that the two of you haven't really made the commitment, that you're not taking this wedding seriously.

DILLON. I don't see how we could take it more seriously!

FAY. Doesn't our abstinence prove just how serious we are?

PASTOR. It proves that you're taking your Bible, or worse, your Bible School teachings, at face value, that you're not even considering the institution of marriage as a practical, everyday, same as it ever was, mundane situation. That it means more than sharing your lives and your mortgages and your bad days and your tremendously awful days and your really horrifically lousy days and your toenails and your M&Ms together—it means sharing your bed together! Do either of you two know what that means? No, of course you can't, because you haven't had sex!

FAY. But... we have had sex.

PASTOR. You have?

DILLON. Yes, of course.

PASTOR. But you said—

FAY. Well, not with each other.

PASTOR. Beg your pardon?

FAY. Dillon and I have had scads of sex, but we're saving ourselves now for each other.

PASTOR. This doesn't make any sense.

DILLON. It makes perfect sense. Both Fay and I have led reasonably fruitful lives—

FAY. Sex, sex, sex...

DILLON. —But when we met each other, we both knew we had found the one, so—

FAY. So, we decided to abstain, to make our wedding day that much more special.

JACKIE. That's beautiful.

PASTOR. That's weird.

JAROD. Sounds weird to me too, but I'm not the one getting married.

PASTOR. Well, I suppose I'm not the one getting married either.

JAROD. And I can't think of two people who belong together more.

JACKIE. Me neither.

FAY. *(Looking at DILLON.)* Me neither.

*(Pause.)*

PASTOR. Okay. You're obviously in love. You want to spend the rest of your lives together. You both have some sort of strange affinity for overwrought Biblical passages. Fine. But in this day and age, why do you want to get *married*?

*(DILLON and FAY look at each other for a moment, then:)*

DILLON and FAY. The presents.

PASTOR. The presents?

JAROD and JACKIE. Why else would anyone get married?

PASTOR. I see. Yes, I see.... And frightfully, I understand. This wedding has my complete and utter blessing, and the four of you have a dinner to get to. Let's run it down one more time, just for luck.

*(Groans, and the PASTOR holds his hands up to squelch their objections. As the PASTOR narrates, the others act out the scenario.)*

PASTOR. Okay, family enters, Mother over here, other Mother over here, Bridesmaids-slash-Groomsmen, very nice—*(Pointing to JACKIE and JAROD.)* You two, in step, good, now Father-of-the-Bride leads in the Bride, everyone stands, she's crying, his tux is too tight, Groom and Bride center themselves around me, I greet, I pray, everyone be seated. *(Pointing to JAROD, then JACKIE.)* Old Testament over here conjures up the holy spirit, followed by

Mrs., I mean, Miss Fire and Brimstone, who brings the house down. I chat lightly with the convened to explain just how much matrimony means in the eyes of the church, everyone's enthralled, this couple is an example to us all, et cetera, do you take so-and-so to be your lawful whatever to love, honor and obey—

FAY and DILLON. Cherish!

PASTOR. Cherish, lovely, does anyone object, let's hope not and I now pronounce you *husband* and wife. Snappy guitar music from the bohemian in the fold-out chair next to the video tripod. The wedding party exits, stepping lively, and there you have it.

JAROD. What about the kiss?

PASTOR. Right. The kiss. You may now kiss the Bride. Go ahead, give it a good trial run.

*(DILLON and FAY stare at each other.*
*They move closer, but are blocked by DILLON's nose.*
*They counter and are blocked by FAY's nose.*
*FINALLY, they tentatively kiss as if for the first time.)*

PASTOR. (Continued.) Mazel tov.

*(Blackout.)*

**END OF PLAY**

# AFTER

by

## Carol K. Mack

## AFTER
### by Carol K. Mack

Directed by Sandra Grand
Dramaturg: Abby Weintraub

*Cindy:* Shelley Kay Wollert
*Glynda:* Brook Hanemann

Stage Manager: Megan L. Kelly
Assistant Stage Manager: Omar Kamal
Costume Designer: Kevin R. McLeod
Lighting Designers: Michele Gallenstein, Brian Shippey
Sound Designer: Shane Rettig
Properties Designer: Mark Walston

## CHARACTERS

Cindy — a journalist
Glynda — a fairy

## SETTING

A field near the parking lot in a remote corner of Disney World.
It is defined by light. A sense of vast space beyond should house
the two actors.

## SOUND

Cartoon music, fairy music,
munchkin giggles.

## AFTER

*(PRECURTAIN: A medley of cartoon music is interrupted by a loudspeaker announcement.)*

TOUR BUS DRIVER. *(Voice-over.)* Right over here, folks! That's all, folks! Let's go ... time's up. Back on the bus now, boys and girls, we've got *lots* more to see! Hi! Step right up ... Hi there. How're ya doin' ... everybody here? Aaalll aboard! ... Hello? ExCUSE me, Miss. HEY, you over there? Hello?! We're boarding ... Lady?! Hey, you can't go over there! Ma'am ... Nobody's *allowed* over there ... HEY! Hey *you*, get back here!

*(During above, CINDY enters, alert, but casual, then, aware she's off-limits, she runs across stage. She wears baseball cap, jeans, knapsack, sneakers, sunglasses and I.D. tag from tour. CINDY is slightly gruff, down-to-earth, independent, bright.)*

TOUR BUS DRIVER. *(Voice-over. Very hostile to way out-of-control.)* Somebody get that visitor. She's off-limits! GET HER! GET HER!

*(During above noise: Offstage shouts, horns, a bewildered CINDY runs across and flees offstage. GLYNDA enters, dressed in a technicolor uniform, and too-high heels, chases her, wobbly. Sparkledust falls in GLYNDA's wake, then a harp strum as she exits in delicate pursuit. CINDY darts back across, looking behind her, then skids to a stop. The cyclorama lights up and there's a "new dawning" sound as CINDY looks straight out, amazed.)*

CINDY. *(Awestruck, looks out to back of house.)* Oh! ... WHOA! *(Lowers her sunglasses, removes cap.)* What the ...

GLYNDA. *(Sweetly, out of breath.)* *There* you are!

CINDY. Where?!

GLYNDA. *(Graciously.)* Off-limits, I fear but ...

CINDY. What *is* this *place*!?

GLYNDA. Please come with me now, dear.

CINDY. *(Grabs GLYNDA's wrist, points to rear of house.)* What's that?!

GLYNDA. What ... ?

CINDY. Who *are* they?

GLYNDA. Come along please?

CINDY. They're all over the grass!

GLYNDA. It's not real grass, it's... (all right)

CINDY. All over!

GLYNDA. This isn't part of the tour.

CINDY. As far as the eye can see!

GLYNDA. It's not for Visitors ...

CINDY. *(Confrontational.)* Why not? Why is it Not For Visitors?

GLYNDA. *(Whispering.)* He wouldn't like it.

CINDY. Who?

GLYNDA. Mr. Walt.

CINDY. Walt ... ? *(Peering at GLYNDA.)* But he's ...

GLYNDA. Yes! But he still *cares.*

CINDY. *(Is she crazy?)* Oh yeah?

GLYNDA. He doesn't like our visitors to be unhappy. Look how upset you're getting. And for what?

CINDY. For what?! You see them? There must be *hundreds* of white horses ...

GLYNDA. This is an unscheduled stop and we must disclaim any ...

CINDY. *(Finally completely realizing.)* *This* is where they all wind up, isn't it?

GLYNDA. *(Simply, GLYNDA the Good.)* Oh my, oh my, oh my.

CINDY. And all of those couples were princes and princesses?

GLYNDA. *Are* princes. Are! We can't *have* this!

CINDY. *(Into her recorder, a reporter.)* Hundreds of white horses have fallen here along with their riders and they're all gorgeous!

GLYNDA. Oh no!

CINDY. The women are dressed up in, *(Squinting.)* prom dresses. Many have blond braids.

GLYNDA. *(Aghast.)* You're a journalist!

CINDY. All the guys are hunks in helmets ...

GLYNDA. Forget you saw this please, for your own sake! For your *species*!

CINDY. *(Into recorder.)* They all appear to be smiling expectantly, as if ...

GLYNDA. It had to end! Try to understand, it had to end!

CINDY. *(Childlike anger.)* WHY!? It says Happily Ever After!

GLYNDA. *(Brightly.)* That's *right,* dear!

CINDY. That's RIGHT?!

GLYNDA. *(With a sweeping gesture accompanied by stardust.)* Why yes! This *is* Happily Ever After.

CINDY. This is IT? A dump site!? *(To her recorder darkly.)* They're all just *laying* there, thick as penguins, far as the eye can see.

GLYNDA. But happily.

CINDY. You call that happily!?

GLYNDA. Goodness, yes. They're just ... *(A rainbow gesture.)* Over.

CINDY. That's not *fair.*

*(CINDY unexpectedly bursts into tears.)*

GLYNDA. Go ahead and cry if it makes you feel better!

*(GLYNDA hands CINDY a twinkling handkerchief.)*

CINDY. *(Crying.)* It's ... I always thought that *after* was only the Beginning. I thought they'd go a long way after After!

GLYNDA. Oh dear, I know. But you see nothing was written for them.

CINDY. What?

GLYNDA. Just: "The End."

CINDY. *(Explosively ranting.)* That's not fair! After they worked so hard? With the *moats* and the monsters, all the dragons and the *towers* and hacking through bramble with *witches* flying after them and does the slipper fit or doesn't it and then finally *finally* it's all okay and what!? They wind up sprawled all over some stupid theme park in Florida!? That is sick!

GLYNDA. *(Beat, then lamely.)* It's sunny. *(At CINDY's look.)* And you can see they're all quite ... content.

CINDY. Forty acres of horses and lovers ... *(Thought, turns dismayed to GLYNDA.)* Oh no! I bet they didn't even... (get a chance.)

GLYNDA. Into the sunset! Hoofbeats, anticipation! A brief and shining moment. En route. It does keep them smiling. Forever. *(Lamely.)* Jellybean?

CINDY. No thanks. I just lost my appetite.

GLYNDA. This isn't an easy job for me either, being a part-time guide here!

CINDY. ... You an actress?

GLYNDA. A fairy.

CINDY. *(Flatly.)* A fairy.

GLYNDA. An unemployed fairy.

CINDY. Oh yeah?

GLYNDA. You couldn't tell?

CINDY. No, actually, I never met one before.

GLYNDA. So you think!

CINDY. Right. Do I get three wishes or what?

GLYNDA. That's *genies!* That's what I mean! Fairies are completely misunderstood and it's impossible to find work. A tooth here, a tooth there ... *We* are the endangered species nobody talks about. Children ignore our random acts of kindness. Cynics abound. Our forests are cut down and we have nowhere left to go. There are horrible waves in the air from your new-fangled inventions! Oh, how we used to dance to the music of the wind-up Victrola as it wafted gently to the bottom of the garden. And now? We get struck down by words flying through the ether like arrows! "You've got mail!" A million times a night! And what does it *mean* anyhow? *(Disdainfully.)* And the New Age? They've got their angels and their channels but what about us? Nobody cares. You think *you're* disillusioned? I'm disenchanted! I wish I could cry. Fairies can't cry you know. Of course you don't know! Why would you? *(Breaking down.)* Now all I can get is "After"! And it's not even supposed to *exist.* It's strictly Off-Limits ... after all these millennia, I'm NOWHERE!

CINDY. I'm really sorry ... I don't know what to *say* ... *(Looks at her uniform I.D. tag.)* "Glynda". Should I clap? Would that help?

GLYNDA. That doesn't work. Applause and barking and car horns all scare us to death. And by the way, we hate caraway seeds.

CINDY. Oh. Then, well what can I do?

GLYNDA. Just make up your mind! *(At puzzled look, pointedly.)* Before you go back to the Bus.

CINDY. *(Jolted back to reality.)* Bus.

GLYNDA. *(Coaching.)* Your *Beau* on the Bus?

CINDY. Oh ... *(Remembering problem.)* Him. Right.

GLYNDA. Yes *him*! That was why you wandered off, wasn't it?

CINDY. Yeah, I guess it was ... It's such a big commitment! I mean I don't know if I can go through with it. I just ...

GLYNDA. You must decide!

CINDY. Well, if this is Happily Ever After, you know what you can do with it!

GLYNDA. Well, if you've decided against a wedding celebration, I'll just fade out now.

CINDY. Wait! I, I didn't say that. All I said was I don't *know* ...

GLYNDA. Tell me: Does he have a horse?

CINDY. No, they don't ride horses anymore *(With grudging belief.)* Glynda.

GLYNDA. *(Wistfully.)* Things change.

CINDY. Yes!

GLYNDA. But fairies don't. Neither do fairytales.

*(Tiny ping sound.)*

CINDY. *(At ping, small fond smile.)* ... He's got a Jeep Wrangler.

GLYNDA. Ah.

*(Tiny ping sound.)*

CINDY. It was really mine and I sold it to him. That's how we met. See I was selling my car to finance a trip to Nepal and this guy shows up to buy it and then, well we wound up going trekking together and, he's really, uh ... *(Doesn't say "great," but her recall is positive, romantic.)* He's ... we've got a lot in common and ... y'know he's a journalist too ... in fact, he's covering this place ... I mean not *this*! *(Stops abruptly, staring at field, realizing.)* So, you gotta write you *own* After. That's the deal, huh?

GLYNDA. Exactly!

CINDY. *(Gesturing to field.)* It's gotta be better than ...

GLYNDA. It *could* be!

CINDY. *(Getting her point.)* Yeah ... It *could* be anything! Right?

GLYNDA. Right!

*(A small ping.)*

CINDY. Thank you! I want to go back now!

GLYNDA. Good! *(As CINDY turns.)* But you can't take anything with you.

CINDY. What do you mean?!

GLYNDA. Memory. We can't let you ...

CINDY. Look, I swear I won't print the story, okay?

GLYNDA. It's too dangerous. It would end your species.

CINDY. Okay, okay, but you can't make me forget!

GLYNDA. Don't force me to do anything unkind.

CINDY. Now what are you, a *hit* fairy?

GLYNDA. *(Touches CINDY with wand, immediate effect. CINDY freezes in place. Casts spell with wand.)* Now, forget this

field and all tale-spinning, the horse, and all the princes grinning.
Forget The End and make a *new* beginning! Forget the pumpkins,
the mice, and all witchcrafter, forget it all in love and laughter.
Forget, and keep your dream of After.

*(Ping.)*

CINDY. *(Opens her eyes, slight disorientation.)* Hello? ... I
thought I ... Excuse me? Where's the bus!?

GLYNDA. It worked! *There* you are, we were just getting worried about you. I'm your tour guide, Glynda?

CINDY. Don't I know you from ... ?

GLYNDA. The Bus. We must hurry. There's a nice young man
on line who's waiting for you ...

CINDY. *(Face brightens.)* Oh yeah, *him*! We're getting *married* this weekend!

GLYNDA. How lovely! I'll be there ... *(Correcting her slip.)* in
spirit.

CINDY. *(Disoriented.)* I feel like, like I forgot something.

GLYNDA. Like a toothbrush? Here. I carry extras.

CINDY. Thanks ... Did you see a tape recorder anywhere?

GLYNDA. Is this yours? *(Handing her recorder with tape dan-
gling.)* I think it... dropped.

CINDY. *(As jellybeans fall from tape recorder.)* Where did *they*
come from? *(Shaking her head.)* I'm feeling kinda weird.

GLYNDA. *(Steering her away from site.)* Probably something
you ate in the cafeteria. Did you eat an apple? Don't worry it's just
a spell ... Now what did you say your name was?

CINDY. Cindy?

*(As they exit.)*

GLYNDA. Cindy! Ah, I knew a Cindy once upon a time, long
long ago ...

**END OF PLAY**

# LUNCHTIME

by

## Rob Marcato

## LUNCHTIME
### by Rob Marcato

Directed by Michael Bigelow Dixon
Dramaturg: Ilana M. Brownstein

*Donna:* Sara Kmack
*Angela:* Kerry Mulvaney
*Man:* Chris Petrelli
*Diners*: Andrea Whitley Clark, Matt Meyer

Scenic Designer: Tom Burch
Costume Designer: Annelise B. Beeckman
Lighting Designers: Karen Hornberger, Matt Shuirr
Sound Designer: Jeremy Lee
Properties Designer: Craig Grigg
Stage Managers: John Armstrong, Catherine A. Kemp

## CHARACTERS

ANGELA, approaching thirty
DONNA, early to mid-twenties
MAN

## SETTING

A food court or public cafeteria at lunch time
in the business district of a major city.

# LUNCHTIME

*(A food court or large, public cafeteria—the seating area of small tables and chairs. It's lunch hour in the business district of a major city.*

*ANGELA and DONNA are about halfway through lunch. The cafeteria is moderately crowded at this hour, but they are in their usual corner which is relatively empty. They sit at a small table. Two or more tables are on stage, but empty. The two women are dressed nicely, in office attire. ANGELA clearly spends time on her looks (hair, make-up, clothes). DONNA spends less, but is pretty in her own natural way.*

*The lights come up. After a short silence, DONNA speaks.)*

DONNA. So, should I ask about last night or—

ANGELA. Oh God, please don't. *(Pause.)* You know, it wouldn't bother me half as much if he gave me a reason. You know, like "I'm coming off a painful breakup and I don't want to rush into things" or "I've had a perpetual headache for the past month" or "My sister has a schnauzer that's more attractive than you"—

DONNA. Angela.

ANGELA. No, I know. *(Beat.)* And you know me, I'm all for taking things slow. In fact, I'm usually on the other side of this. But this isn't taking it slow. We're not moving. We're in Park.

DONNA. What happened?

ANGELA. What happened? What always happens. He came over. I cooked for him. I mean, I *cooked* for him—an indication of the depths of desperation to which I have sunk. We ate, we talked. We sat on my couch, we talked. It was lovely. A bottle of wine was consumed, mostly by me. I'm sending him signals strong enough to attract a small army. Then, all of a sudden it's "I've had a wonderful time, but I have to get up for work tomorrow," as if I don't, a kiss on the forehead and out the door.

DONNA. I'm sorry.

ANGELA. Oh God, then this morning—

DONNA. I heard.

ANGELA. Fucking Meyerson stomps in after his nine o'clock presentation which apparently did not go too well because he's ranting and raving that I didn't do the margins and spacing the way he asked for them, which of course I did, like bigger margins are gonna hide the fact that he's a clueless schmuck. *(Beat.)* So, naturally, I've been a powerhouse bitch to everyone this morning. And now you're stuck listening to me bitch about it.

DONNA. No, that's what I'm here for. If you can't bitch to me, who can you bitch to.

ANGELA. Well, thank you, but I don't know how you put up with me.

DONNA. *(Beat.)* I sorta tune you out and just smile and nod my head a lot.

*(DONNA smiles.)*

ANGELA. *(Looks up surprised. Then, laughing.)* That was good. I'm proud of you.

DONNA. Thanks. *(Beat.)* One good thing about today though. Your little friend isn't here.

ANGELA. I was about to say. It looks like he won't be joining us today. Maybe I should ask *him* out. At least I know he'd *listen* to me. Though, I think *you're* the one he's got a thing for.

DONNA. Don't even joke about that.

*(They laugh. Pause. Then, ANGELA notices MAN coming toward them, but offstage.)*

ANGELA. Oh, see now, we had to go and talk about him. We couldn't leave well enough alone.

DONNA. What, is he here?

ANGELA. Uh huh.

*(MAN enters, stops, and looks over the available tables. He is dressed plainly, in a button-down shirt and slacks. He holds a tray of food, with a newspaper tucked under his arm. The following narration pretty closely matches MAN's actions.)*

ANGELA. Hmmm. Now, let's see. Where ever shall I sit today? Oh, lookey there. Out of all these tables, why don't I choose the one right next to those two women over there, so I can inconspicuously eavesdrop on their conversation. *(MAN moves to a table behind DONNA and sits in its only chair, with his back to the women. Then, he remembers something and stands.)* Oh! I mustn't forget the extra chair for my imaginary friend who will never join me.

*(He takes a chair from a nearby table, places it across from his, then sits again and begins eating and reading. ANGELA and DONNA talk in low voices.)*

DONNA. He'll hear you.

ANGELA. Well, that's what he wants, isn't it?

DONNA. Do you really think he ...

ANGELA. Oh, come on. Once is a fluke, twice is a coincidence, but this is getting ridiculous.

DONNA. Okay, I'll admit he sits next to us a lot, but that doesn't mean he's listening to us.

ANGELA. Then what's he doing—enjoying our perfume?

DONNA. I don't know. I just think we're being a little paranoid. He seems pretty harmless to me.

ANGELA. My lovely, charming, naïve, trusting friend. You are a stalker's dream. *(Beat.)* Am I gonna have to prove this to you? *(Beat.)* Here. Watch him.

DONNA. What?

ANGELA. *(Motioning for DONNA to turn towards MAN.)* Watch him. *(DONNA covertly looks at him. Then, in a louder voice.)* So, I heard this great new joke this morning. What's the difference between a lightbulb and a pregnant woman?

DONNA. *(Beat. Then, realizing it's her cue.)* Oh, uh, what?

ANGELA. You can't unscrew a pregnant woman. *(Both DONNA and ANGELA laugh. Man laughs silently so that his shoulders shake slightly.)* Did you see that?

DONNA. What?

ANGELA. His shoulders shook. *(Beat.)* He was laughing. His little, narrow shoulders shook, and so did his hand and the paper.

DONNA. Maybe a little. You did say it pretty loud, though.

ANGELA. Oh, come on. He was listening to us.

DONNA. Okay, fine. So let's say he's listening to us.

ANGELA. He is.

DONNA. Okay. So, what can we do about it? Do you want to move?

ANGELA. No. We shouldn't have to move. This is our table. We sit here every day.

DONNA. Well, I agree. But, I mean, what can we do about it then?

ANGELA. *(Beat.)* I'm gonna say something to him.

DONNA. What?

ANGELA. I'm gonna tell the fucker not to sit here anymore.

DONNA. Angela.

ANGELA. *(To MAN.)* Excuse me.

DONNA. Angela.

ANGELA. Excuse me. *(MAN turns to face them, and DONNA looks down at her lap, embarrassed.)* Hi. Um... my friend and I were wondering if you could ... you know, sit someplace else.

MAN. Excuse me?

ANGELA. You know. Sit ... not near us.

MAN. I'm sorry, I don't ... I don't think I—

ANGELA. Oh, come on. I'm sure you don't mean any harm, but we know what you're doing.

MAN. What I'm ... I don't understand what—

ANGELA. You know—listening.

MAN. *(Beat.)* Well, I don't know what you're implying, but I certainly—

ANGELA. *(Forcefully.)* Okay, stop playing dumb. Could you please go sit somewhere else.

MAN. *(Beat.)* Listen, I don't know what I did to you, but ... This is my seat. I have a right to sit here. You can ... I have a right to sit here.

*(MAN turns back to his paper.)*

ANGELA. *(She stares at him in frustration and disbelief. Then, throwing in the towel.)* Okay, fine. You win. Sit there. Listen to our conversation. *(Under her breath.)* Fuckin' stalker.

*(MAN hears this, and is clearly unsettled by it. He turns to AN-GELA.)*

MAN. *(Timid, but angry.)* You're very rude.

*(Back to his paper.)*

ANGELA. *(Looking up.)* Excuse me?

DONNA. Angela.

ANGELA. Hey! I'm rude? I'm "very rude"? What, eavesdropping on other people's conversations doesn't qualify as rude?

MAN. *(Looking up, adamant.)* I don't ... I don't do that.

ANGELA. Oh, you don't, do you? *(She walks quickly to him, snatches the paper out of his hands, and moves to the other side of his table.)* Okay. Then tell me something from today's news.

MAN. Could you please give me my paper back?

ANGELA. Come on. Just one story. One headline. One picture. Tell me one thing you perused while you weren't desperately trying to hear every word we said.

MAN. I ... I don't have to ... Could you please—

ANGELA. You can't, can you? No. But I bet you can tell me the difference between a lightbulb and a pregnant woman, can't you?

MAN. Listen. Could you please leave me alone?

ANGELA. Oh, I'm sorry. Am I sitting in someone's seat?

MAN. Well ... yes.

ANGELA. Who are you waiting for? A ladyfriend?

MAN. That's none of your business.

ANGELA. Ooooh, a ladyfriend. I'd love to meet her. I think I'll just stay here until she comes.

MAN. Why are you doing this to me? I haven't done anything to you.

ANGELA. You sit here every day and listen to our conversations. Don't you see anything wrong with that?

MAN. I haven't hurt you, have I?

ANGELA. These are *our* conversations—the intimate details of *our* lives. They are not for *you*. Go find your own.

*(ANGELA starts to return to her table.)*

MAN. You are cruel.

*(ANGELA stops.)*

ANGELA. *(Hands on the back of the empty chair.)* At least I don't have to eat alone.

MAN. You are a cruel person.

ANGELA. *(Pushing the chair until it hits the table.)* At least I'm not waiting for imaginary friends.

MAN. *(A warning.)* Don't push me.

ANGELA. *(Pushing the chair and table into him.)* Friends that will never fucking come!

MAN. *(Beat. Then, awkwardly, but with real venom.)* I wish your boyfriend would just fuck you and get it over with so you could stop taking your frustrations out on other people. If only he could get it up with you in the room. Have you tried putting a bag over your head? That might help.

*(Pause. ANGELA is stunned at first. Then, shock turns to fury.)*

ANGELA. You son of a bitch!

*(ANGELA runs at him and falls onto him, beating him with flailing arms. He curls into a ball with his hands on top of his head, repeating "I'm sorry" over and over again. DONNA goes to them, and does her best to pull ANGELA off him. She is able to do so. ANGELA stands for a moment, stunned, then runs offstage. DONNA watches her exit, looks back over the room, also stunned, then starts after ANGELA. MAN moans in pain, holding his hands to his forehead. DONNA hears him, stops, and turns to look at him.)*

DONNA. *(Beat.)* Are you okay?
MAN. It's only a scratch, I think.
DONNA. Let me see.

*(MAN gingerly removes his hands from his forehead. From a few feet away, DONNA examines it. There is a large, red scratch on his forehead.)*

DONNA. Ooh, she really got you there.
MAN. She has long nails.

*(DONNA deliberates for a moment, looks offstage where ANGELA exited, then back at MAN.)*

DONNA. Here. *(She takes a napkin from her table and dips it in her water. Then, moving tentatively to him, she cleans the scratch with the napkin and presses on it.)* I'm really sorry about that.
MAN. It's not your fault. You're very kind. *(Beat.)* Why are you friends with her?
DONNA. Oh. She's not all bad. I mean, she's had a rough life, but she's got a big heart and she's very good to me.
MAN. I love that about you. No matter what, you always manage to see the good in people.

*(DONNA steps back from him.)*

DONNA. I really should go make sure she's okay.

*(DONNA starts to leave.)*

MAN. Donna! *(She turns to him.)* Uh ... I was just wondering if ... you know, sometime you might want to ... or if you and I could ... I was just—

DONNA. Are you asking me out?

MAN. *(Desperately explaining.)* It wasn't supposed to be like that. I mean, I'm not supposed to be like that. I'm not like that, or at least I haven't been for a long time.

DONNA. You just insulted my friend, and now you're asking me out?

*(DONNA rushes to pick up her bag and ANGELA's.)*

MAN. Listen, I don't care about her, I care about you. I would never do that to you. *(As DONNA exits.)* I would never hurt you.

*(Man is left alone. Lights down.)*

**END OF PLAY**

# TATTOO

by

**Jane Martin**

# TATTOO

*(Three women in their 20s sit on chairs facing a door upstage. LINK [short for Linchovna] is dressed in black slacks, has short blond hair, several earrings and all ten fingers adorned with rings. JENNY is dressed in a suit as a young advertising account executive might for a date. JONES is more in the girly-girl vein with curly hair and Laura Ashley style. She is a graduate student who works also as a waitress.)*

JENNY. What time is it?

JONES. *(Very Southern.)* 7:45.

JENNY. Where is this guy?

LINK. *(A Russian accent.)* He will come. He is sister's ex-husband. Very reliable person. He will come.

JONES. But ... like if they both ... I mean what do we do if, you know, they both ...

LINK. Very reliable.

JONES. I am sweating like a shot-putter.

JENNY. Calm down. Breathe. *(Knock.)* See.

JONES. But what if it's ...

LINK. Is Vladimir. Very Russian knock. Okay? I get.

JONES. But if it's William, do we ...

LINK. Only Russian is knocking so deliberate as this. You sit, I do. *(She goes to the door.)* Ah. *(Russian.)* Ooh m$^{ie}$yáh b $^{ih}$ll pree-páh-dok syáird-tsuh. Tih uh-púz-dah-vá-yesh. (You gave me a heart attack. You are late.)

VLADIMIR. *(Russian.)* Ahv-tóe-booss pree-shóal púhz-dnuh. Yah lóohch-shuh dyéluhl shtaw smúg. (Bus was late. I did the best I could.) *(He enters. He is big, very big, and bearded and tattooed. He has a bag with him much like an old-fashioned doctor bag.)* (K)huh-ruh-sháw, éh-tut ch$^{ie}$l-uh-v$^{ie}$k gdyeh aown. (Okay, this guy he is where?)

JONES. My God, he's speaking Russian

87

LINK. He *is* Russian. All Russians are coming to your country, get ready. *(Russian.)* Aown n'ee yesh-cháw n'ee pree-yéh-(k)hull. Ee-dée zhdoo féh-toy k^wóm-nah-tuh. (He hasn't arrived. Go in that room and wait.)

VLADIMIR. *(Russian.)* (K) huh-ruh-sháw n^ao^w ooh m^ie n-yáh svee-dáh-nyuh ch'ée-ez chahss. Éh-tuh dvair? (Okay, but in one hour I have an appointment. That door?)

*(VLADIMIR heads toward the other room.)*

LINK. *(Russian.)* Da. (Yes.)

JENNY. What did you tell him?

LINK. Be ready. We will tell him when. Call him in.

JONES. Is this really a good idea? Is this really, really, really a good idea?

JENNY. We need closure. He needs closure. There is going to be closure.

*(A knock on the door.)*

JONES. *(Whispering.)* Oh my God. Oh my God it's him. I have a good idea. You guys do this. You'll be better at this than me. I'll just ... oh my God, can I do this?

LINK. Sit down. Not to vacillate. We do this. *(They arrange themselves on the chairs.)* Okay. Very calm. Very good. This is no more than result of his actions. We are a living logic for him. Breathing. Breathing. Good. Okay. We begin. *(Another knock.)* I am liking this.

*(She opens the door. The man outside, WILLIAM, immediately grabs her and pulls her into a passionate kiss. After it has gone on for awhile, he has the sense of being watched. He removes his lips from LINK and sees the seated woman.)*

WILLIAM. Oh shit.

JENNY. Hello, William.

JONES. Hi.

LINK. *(Still in his arms.)* Hello, William.

WILLIAM. *(Trying to recover.)* All right, all right, this is really ... an intrusion. This is really second-rate is what it is. I cannot believe ... have I ever gone through your purses, have I ever gone through ...

JENNY. You were going to say "our drawers?"

WILLIAM. No, no, I wasn't, Jenny, I wasn't going to say "your drawers." I was pointing out that there are issues of privacy, that there are questions of trust ... *(Realizes he is still embracing LINK.)* Oh. Excuse me. *(He releases her.)* I was so ...

JENNY. Fucked up.

WILLIAM. No, not fucked up, Jenny, taken aback. Yes. Completely taken aback that you ...

JENNY. Knew each other.

WILLIAM. No. I didn't say ... you are putting, unfairly, words in my mouth. Look Jenny, if you are looking for the negative, you will find the negative. If you insist something is shoddy, it will look shoddy to you.

JONES. My daddy will come down here and eat your lunch!

WILLIAM. Jones, will you for once in your life wait to start crying until there is something to cry about?

JONES. You slept with me at 6A.M. this morning!

WILLIAM. Well, yes I did, Jones. I did that. Well, actually, it was around 6:15.

JENNY. So that was the early meeting?

WILLIAM. Well no, I mean yes, there was an early meeting ...

JONES. You said you had to see me. You said you were wracked with desire.

LINK. Wracked with desire?

JENNY. You said that to me at lunch.

WILLIAM. Okay, hold it ...

JENNY. It's why I went into the trees with you in the park.

LINK. "Wracked with desire," yes, it's very charming.

WILLIAM. Excuse me ...

LINK. In the trees his methodology is what?

JENNY. Kissed my neck.

JONES. That's it! That's what he does! He goes for your goddamn neck like an attack dog! And here I was thinking that was because he was wracked with desire!

LINK. Then hand goes up leg. He is then unbuttons the blouse...

JONES. Then he starts saying "please," he says "please" over and over and over! Please, please, please!

LINK. Is like puppy.

WILLIAM. All right, goddamnit, I concede the point!

JENNY. He "concedes" the point.

WILLIAM. If the point is that I am having more than one relationship, you can get off that point because nobody is arguing with you!

JENNY. Oh good.

WILLIAM. We can calm down!

JENNY. Fine.

JONES. You made love to me at 6 A.M. this morning! You called me your little tuna melt!

JENNY. Tuna melt?

LINK. What is tuna melt?

JENNY. You took me behind the trees at noon.

LINK. And tonight you will teach me Kama Sutra.

WILLIAM. This isn't about sex. This is about something way more profound than sex.

JENNY. Oh good, because I thought it *was* about sex.

WILLIAM. Well, it isn't, Jenny, it's about ...

JENNY. Screwing like a rabbit.

WILLIAM. No.

JENNY. Completely indiscriminate sex.

LINK. Altogether impersonal.

JENNY. Wildly dysfunctional.

JONES. He called me his "tuna melt."

JENNY. Okay, Jones, that adds a dollop of romance.

WILLIAM. You may not recognize this but it's about *passion*. It is a frank admission that complex personalities have complex needs, and that ...

JENNY. Point of order.

WILLIAM. Each of those needs finds passionate fulfillment ...

JENNY. Point of order.

WILLIAM. What?

JENNY. You are the complex personality in question?

WILLIAM. Yes, I am.

JENNY. Just trying to keep up.

WILLIAM. Now each one of you is very different.

JENNY. We are very different.

WILLIAM. And in each case a different part of me responds. I don't give the same thing, I don't get the same thing. The me that is with each of you could not respond to the others. That self is faithful and would never betray you. You wouldn't want that part of me you don't have, and were I not as complex as I am there wouldn't have been enough of each part of me for you to relate to, to care about, in fact, to love.

*(There is a long, stunned pause.)*

JONES. What the *hell* is he talking about?

LINK. He has many souls.

JENNY. He da three-souled man.

WILLIAM. Go ahead, Jenny, make fun of what you don't understand. You are a wonderful person, a very talented advertising

account executive, but you have a demeaningly reductive view of life. That is one of the reasons your spirit has sought me out. You want to be carried into deeper water.

JENNY. Well, I will admit that it's getting pretty deep.

WILLIAM. Now I'm not saying there aren't issues here. Matters of the heart, intimacies that I want to discuss with you alone, Jenny, and you too Jones, of course I meant you, too.

JONES. Okay now, I want to get down and talk some Georgia talk here ... you know, get right on down in the red dirt here ... and what I got on my mind is "am I *is* or am I *ain't* your Tuna Melt?"

WILLIAM. I am what you need me to be, Jones. *(LINK locks the door.)* What are you doing, Link?

LINK. I am making here old-fashioned totalitarian state.

JENNY. *(Moving one chair away from the others.)* Sit down, William.

WILLIAM. I see no reason to sit down.

JENNY. Bill, do you remember when we very recently began seriously to make our wedding plans?

WILLIAM. Yes, I do.

JENNY. Do you remember saying you wanted a really big wedding?

WILLIAM. Yes I do.

JENNY. And I said, "Honey, I just don't know that many people," and you said, "Sweetie, I could list two hundred family, friends and business associates right now." And I bet you ten dollars and, by golly, you sat right down and did it!

LINK. He has good organizational memory, to do *this* he had to have such a memory.

JENNY. *(Taking a paper out of her briefcase.)* Now, Bill, this is the account of your activities today that I plan to fax to that list if you don't sit down. *(He glances over the letter and sits down.)* I know it's a little heavy on sexual specifics, but you have such a remarkably individual style I thought it made good reading.

JONES. I am never dressing up like that again at 6 A.M.!

WILLIAM. What precisely is it that you want?

LINK. Ah.

JENNY. Ah.

JONES. Ah.

JENNY. What precisely? Well, we want you to meet someone.

LINK. *(Russian.)* Vlah-dée-meer, vuh-(k)huh-dée! Puh-ráh rahbᵃoʷ-táhts. (Vladimir, come in! It is time to go to work.) *(VLADIMIR enters.)* Vladimir, I am wanting you to meet interesting person William. William, this is interesting person Vladimir.

*(VLADIMIR clicks his heels and bows slightly.)*

WILLIAM. If you are planning to kill me or harm me, I would like it to be clearly understood that I am a lawyer, my friends are lawyers, my mother is a lawyer, my brother Don is a *ferocious* lawyer, and you will pay. P-A-Y. Pay.

LINK. I like this, William, this is very dramatic, but in this time we don't kill you. This is very funny idea though. You make good Russian joke. Wait, one moment, I tell Vladimir.

*(In Russian, LINK communicates WILLIAM's fear. VLADIMIR laughs and slaps WILLIAM on the back.)*

JENNY. Okay, so it's "the lady and the tiger." Behind two doors, the choice is yours. Here's the deal. I will fax the aforementioned document to the aforementioned list, or Vladimir will tattoo on your butt our version of what you did today.

*(JENNY hands WILLIAM another piece of paper.)*

WILLIAM. What?!
JONES. Signed.
JENNY. And dated.
WILLIAM. You are kidding.
JENNY. Take a good look at Vladimir. Does he look like he's kidding?

*(VLADIMIR opens his bag, takes out a small towel and begins laying out the tools of his trade.)*

LINK. In Russia this man is thoracic surgeon, but in America he is tattoo artist. Such is fate of Russian people. *(Russian.)* N'ee pláhts, moy droohg. (Do not weep, my friend.)

*(He wipes his eyes.)*

WILLIAM. *(Still holding the paper.)* I am supposed to go through life with this tattooed on my butt?
JENNY. William, like many pharmaceuticals, you need a warning label.
JONES. But they can take a tattoo off.
LINK. Not with Russian inks.
WILLIAM. I cannot believe this is happening to me!
JENNY. So you choose the fax?

WILLIAM. You know perfectly well that would ruin my career.

JENNY. Well, see now, we just seem to be on the horns of a dilemma.

JONES. Your career or your rear.

LINK. The lady ...

JONES. Or your skinny white butt.

WILLIAM. How the hell did the three of you find out about each other?

LINK. Vladimir is also private detective.

WILLIAM. *(To LINK.)* And what made you think you needed a private detective?

LINK. Because, my darling, I am Russian.

JENNY. So what'll it be, Billy?

WILLIAM. Can I have just a goddamn minute here?

JONES. I'm gonna wash your mouth out with soap.

LINK. Man must come to terms with tragic fate. Is good. Okay, while you think, Vladimir will sing you song of suffering and transfiguration from Ukraine. *(VLADIMIR does; it has no words but great feeling.)* And I will read you Kama Sutra.

WILLIAM. Oh God.

LINK. You say tonight our souls, our bodies will become one through Kama Sutra. This I don't want to miss.

*(LINK begins reading the first few sentences of the Kama Sutra. "Man, the period of whose life is one hundred years, should practise Dharma, Artha and Kama at different times and in such a manner that they may harmonize together and not clash in any way. He should acquire learning in his childhood, in his youth and middle age he should attend to Artha and Kama, and in his old age he should perform Dharma, and thus seek to gain Moksha, i.e., release from further transmigration." VLADIMIR sings more softly and prepares, The women watch. WILLIAM fumes and puts his head in his hands.)*

*(Lights Out.)*

**END OF PLAY**

# PRECIPICE

by

## William Mastrosimone

*Dedication: To Rev. Ross Holtz*

### PRECIPICE
### by William Mastrosimone

Directed by Frazier W. Marsh
Dramaturg: Josh Abrams

*SHE:* Allison deLeon
*HE:* Ricardo Frederick Evans

Set Designer: Paul Owen
Costume Designer: Annalise Beeckman
Lighting Designer: Eric Cope
Sound Designer: Dave Preston
Property Designer: Ben Hohman
Stage Manager: Bobbi Masters

### CHARACTERS
He
She
### TIME
An hour before dark in July.
### PLACE
Mount Rainier, Washington.
### SET
A precipice (perhaps the edge of the stage).
A small fir tree.
### COSTUME
Both in hiking boots, shorts, t-shirts, backpacks.
Hers are worn, his are new.
### LIGHTING
Semi-darkness and fog.

## PRECIPICE

*(Sound of wind. Up with diffuse gray light. Enter YOUNG WOMAN. SHE removes her backpack. Enter YOUNG MAN.)*

SHE. Ready?

HE. This the place?

SHE. Absolutely. I remember this tree.

HE. There's only fifty trillion trees around us, and you remember this particular tree.

SHE. The way it grows out of the rock. Unless you want to, I'll jump first.

HE. I've seen a hundred trees growing out of rock.

SHE. No. I remember this curve in the lower trunk, how the north wind must've forced the tree to grow crooked.

HE. Heliotropism. Grows towards the southern exposure.

SHE. That's east.

HE. Can't be east. There's the last light. That's west. So that way has to be south.

*(SHE looks at compass.)*

SHE. Hmmm. You're right. I've gotten turned around by the terrain.

HE. And I'm not an outdoor guy.

SHE. Then you toss the packs over to me. Ready?

HE. Almost..

*(HE takes off one of his boots.)*

SHE. Pebble?

HE. Boots. Too big. Told you I should've gotten a size smaller.

SHE. Not with hiking socks. Are those cotton?

HE. Yeah.

SHE. What happened to the wool socks?

HE. Wool irritates my skin. Makes my feet sweat.

SHE. Wool breathes moisture away. Cotton holds it. "Cold feet—you're beat."

HE. You're just full of those mountaineer sayings.

SHE. Ready?

HE. You sure this is where we jumped over this morning?

SHE. Positive.

HE. Wish I could see the ledge over there.

SHE. Been hiking this trail half my life. You get a cold northwester on a July day, that fog pours off the snow like smoke. *(Consults watch thermometer.)* Since we stopped here it dropped another six degrees. We really have to move.

HE. Let's go.

SHE. You okay about it?

HE. I wish I felt better about it.

SHE. You're not a hundred percent?

HE. I know I can jump the five feet across. Did it this morning.

SHE. But?

HE. It's just—

SHE. Damn fog—

HE. Yeah. I wish I could see the other side.

SHE. *(Picks up a small stone.)* Scientific method. Observe. I'm going to throw a stone. *(Tosses stone across the precipice. We hear it hit rock.)* Q.E.D. Okay?

HE. No.

SHE. Didn't you hear the stone hit the ledge over there?

HE. I heard the stone hit stone. Whether it's the ledge we jumped from I have no idea. And neither do you.

SHE. What else could it be?

HE. I don't know, and neither do you.

*(SHE picks up another stone.)*

SHE. Okay, listen to this stone.

HE. Hey, you could throw stones over all day long but no way I'm jumping where I can't see.

SHE. For one thing, we don't have all day. If we don't jump now, we're gonna get caught in a blizzard.

HE. I still don't think this is where we jumped over. Why'd you pick *this* day? Didn't you listen to a weather report?

SHE. Look, Mount Rainier—

HE. I mean, a meteorologist can see a storm coming.

SHE. Rainier makes its own weather. It's unpredictable. Even after we jump we still have six or seven thousand feet to descend. I really think we need to move on.

HE. Need a break.

*(HE opens his pack, takes out potato chips.)*

SHE. We need to keep ahead of the storm.

HE. My sugar's low.

SHE. Minutes are gonna count. We can eat later.

HE. I feel weak. I need some energy to jump.

SHE. This might do you better. Trail mix.

*(SHE offers him a plastic bag out of her pack.)*

HE. I'll stay with the potato chips.

SHE. All that salt's only gonna make you thirsty. *(HE takes a drink from his canteen, offers it to her; SHE rejects it.)* Which makes you urinate more, which rids you of more electrolytes, which makes you tired.

HE. Excuse me for being human.

SHE. You must've stopped a half a dozen times—

HE. So who's counting?

SHE. Takes a toll, that's all I'm saying. That's why you're tired. All you eat's junk. It's times like these when the discipline pays off.

HE. Times like these I don't need a lecture on health.

SHE. Sorry.

HE. No big deal.

SHE. Actually—nevermind.

HE. What?

SHE. Wanna take a few practice starts and sort of sneak up on it? Let's stretch. C'mon.

HE. My legs are fine. It's my brain.

SHE. If I jumped, would that convince you?

HE. It would convince me you're out of your mind.

SHE. What if I jumped and landed safely?

HE. And what if you're wrong?

SHE. How can I be wrong? Nobody moved the mountain.

HE. You're so cocksure. You won't even consider the possibility you might be mistaken?

SHE. We did it this morning, we can do it again.

HE. And what if you fall to your death?

SHE. C'mon.

HE. Or worse.

SHE. What could be worse?

HE. You fall down in that chasm with a broken back, you're in terrible pain, and I'm up here unable to help.

SHE. I'm prepared for that.

HE. Who could possibly be prepared for that?

SHE. I know anything can happen up here. Rock slide. Avalanche. Run across a grizzly and her cubs. Just stumble and fall. Worse can happen in Seattle.

HE. Would you dash across the street if you were blind?

SHE. It's not the same thing.

HE. You're right. A blind person knows there's the other side of the street. Knows drivers have car brakes.

SHE. Your fear is talking.

HE. Where I come from they call it smarts. This is a helluva first date.

SHE. After I jump, toss the packs over, and toss 'em high. Better to overshoot. Just note where I jump. *(Lays a stone on the ledge.)* Let this be your marker. Jump off that marker. Give yourself enough running space. Measure it out a few times. And remember, jump high. Only bad thing is you sorta come in for a crash landing because you can't see how to break your fall. Okay?

*(SHE stands back to give herself running room.)*

HE. Unbelievable.

SHE. What?

HE. You're really gonna run and leap into the fog not knowing what's over there?

SHE. I know what's over there.

HE. You don't know. You believe. You hope. You wish. You pray. You don't know the difference between what you know and what you hope.

SHE. You heard the stone land on the ledge.

HE. Stone hit stone. Period. That's a typical you-ism. You hope a ledge is there, therefore, a ledge's over there. No! There's rock over there. It may be flat. Or it may be round. It may be vertical. It may be horizontal. It's not a fact because you said it. It's only a fact when I can see it.

SHE. So what do you suggest we do?

HE. I don't know. Find a fallen tree. Make a bridge.

SHE. Brilliant. Trust a tree that's been down for years, full of termites.

HE. This is nuts.

SHE. Nuts will be when that blizzard catches up to us. Nuts is wasting precious time.

HE. We jumped over here to take a shortcut. Why don't we backtrack and go the long way?

SHE. Can't. We'd have to walk two hours right into the storm.

HE. Then we wait out the storm.

SHE. In shorts and t-shirts? A storm like this can have arctic winds up to seventy-five miles per. That's hurricane speed. That's hypothermia. It could dump two, three, four feet of snow on us in six hours. Wet snow. And that's death. We won't survive it. This mountain kills disrespectors. We stay, we die. Horribly.

HE. If you knew there could be blizzards in July up here, why'd you come unprepared?

SHE. I goofed.

HE. Oh—you mean you can be wrong sometimes?

SHE. I'm not wrong about the ledge.

He. You thought east was south—and you're gonna jump?

SHE. Now if you would please get out of my way, I'm gonna prove it to you.

HE. You're so certain.

SHE. Move, please.

He. You're so absolute about what you can't see.

SHE. I know in my heart it's there.

HE. You don't know anything.

SHE. Move.

HE. This is a helluva first date.

SHE. Also the last.

HE. No question about it.

SHE. You're just a cat up a tree. This morning you leaped across laughing. But now your body quits on you, so you start manufacturing reasons not to jump back. You're tired. You're spent. And fear's got the best of you.

HE. *(Imitating her.)* "Hey, wanna take a shortcut?" What was I thinking when I said yes?

SHE. Yeah, what were you thinking?

HE. Never scored on a mountain top before. Thought you wouldn't want to keep seeing a guy who wasn't as crazy as you. So I jumped. Of my own free will. You didn't make me. All the things we said to one another. I thought if I didn't go into your world, and take all the chances, we'd never be close. I didn't know it would kill me. Just go.

SHE. I can't just go. I'm responsible for getting you on this side. Let's hold hands and jump together. C'mon.

HE. What?

SHE. We throw the packs over, stand way, way back, take a running leap across. We can do it.

HE. You're truly out of your mind.

SHE. You may be afraid of that leap now, but when those winds hit you, when you feel your core heat dropping and start hallucinating and all you want t do is sleep, a part of you may come to your senses, but it'll be too late. You'll be even weaker, even more afraid.

HE. Let's make a shelter.

SHE. Out of what?

HE. Trees.

SHE. What trees?

HE. Branches. Anything.

SHE. You think it's easy?

HE. We'll figure it out.

SHE. Lifetime woodsmen would be hard-pressed.

HE. You go on. When you get back, tell 'em where I am.

SHE. I worked Search and Rescue. They don't go out in bad storms. They jeopardize lives for lives to a point. This storm is that point. To get you out of here, they need a six-man foot and dog unit. They have to carry a ten-foot ladder and litter up six thousand feet. The snow will be too deep. They'll wait it out. The helicopter won't fly in a blizzard. Won't fly in winds over forty miles per hour. Maybe they'll come. Maybe they won't. Maybe all they need is a bodybag. Then again, there might be lots of other goofs for S&R to fetch. There's two skeletons hanging from ropes on the southeast precipice. Mountain climbers. Been hanging there for years. Two ribcages, a bit of vertebrae, swinging on the end of a rope in the wind. Nobody can get to them. Swinging in the wind. Back and forth. Untouchable.

HE. Damn.

SHE. You did it before.

HE. That was a lifetime ago.

SHE. It was eight hours ago. You did it before. You can do it again.

HE. This is definitely not the spot. When I jumped over, I scraped my knee.

SHE. So what.

HE. I looked down on rock.

SHE. I'm sorry, I can't listen to anymore of this.

HE. Saw my blood on the rock.

SHE. I have to save my life.

HE. There's no blood on that rock.

SHE. For what it's worth, I've heard it said that freezing's the kindest death. It's painful at first, but after threshold's reached, numbness takes over and all you'll want to do is sleep. Then you'll curl up and fade away.

HE. Who would know that?

SHE. It's a medical fact.

HE. Who came back from the dead to make it a fact?

SHE. Believe what you want to believe. I believe we're being tested.

HE. Don't get mystical on me. I need real.

SHE. I know this trail.

HE. Like east is west. You think you know a lot of things. You say things like "Mount Rainier's holy." It's a big rock, okay? "Rainier makes its own weather." If you knew anything, we'd have the right gear, wouldn't we?

SHE. I'm moving on.

HE. Wrong about south being east.

SHE. Here's my pack.

HE. Why can't you be wrong about the precipice?

SHE. You'll find a windbreaker—

HE. Answer me.

SHE. And some food. I suggest you wait as long as possible before you consume the food—

HE. Moron.

*(SHE picks up a crumpled ball of silver gum-wrapper foil.)*

SHE. This is the spot. You dropped this before. Your gum wrapper.

HE. I picked mine up.

*(HE digs in pocket for several yellow gum-wrappers with their silver foil.)*

SHE. You have four wrappers but only three foils. One's missing. And this is it.

HE. The foil you found's weathered. That's been here.

SHE. Nobody comes here.

HE. We did.

SHE. Then where's the fourth foil?

HE. Probably on my car floor. Or in the ashtray. I put my body where my mouth is. Show me blood on that rock and I'll jump. Right now. Show me. Right now. I'll go first. Just show me.

SHE. I can't.

HE. No, you can't.

SHE. I can only show you by jumping.

HE. Then why don't you? *(Beat.)* Huh? *(Beat.)* Go on. Nobody's in your way.

SHE. I can't now ...

HE. Spooked?

SHE. I was so sure.

HE. Guess what? You're a human being.

SHE. Don't know how this could happen to me.

HE. Damn fog.

SHE. Of all people.

HE. The terrain.

SHE. Yeah.

HE. So what should we do?

SHE. I don't know. Don't know.

*(SHE opens her pack, puts on her windbreaker. SHE sits, eyes fixed on the ledge.)*

HE. I'll look for some firewood.

*(HE starts to exit but stops. Lights begin to fade. HE looks at her. SHE never takes her eyes off the ledge. Lights fade to black.)*

**END OF PLAY**

# SEEING THE LIGHT

by

## Robert McKay

## SEEING THE LIGHT
### by Robert McKay

Directed by Jennifer Hubbard
Dramaturg: Amy Wegener

*Ned:* Chad Hildreth
*Marshall:* Thomas Ward
*Casey:* Ricardo Frederick Evans

Set Designer: Paul Owen
Costume Designer: Annalise Beeckman
Lighting Designer: Eric Cope
Sound Designer: Dave Preston
Properties Designer: Ben Hohman
Stage Manager: Bobbi Masters

### CAST

NED
MARSHALL
CASEY

## SEEING THE LIGHT

*(Two men are seated at a table. One of the men, MARSHALL, is reading a paper or magazine. His feet are up on the table. The other man, NED, is busy playing solitaire. Overhead, as if in the ceiling, is a light. It is not on when the lights come up. After a short time, in which MARSHALL is buried in his reading, and NED is intent on his cards, the light comes on. It is red. Neither man notices the light. Finally, after some time, NED sees that the light is on. He returns to his game, then his attention comes back to the light. He looks at it for a while, almost plays another card, looks back. It's still on. At this point, he speaks.)*

NED. Marshall. *(MARSHALL grunts.)* Marshall, look at that.
MARSHALL. *(Still buried.)* What?
NED. The light.
MARSHALL. *(Not coming out.)* What about the light, Ned?
NED. It's on. *(After a pause, with reluctance, and a show which reveals how little he likes being interrupted, MARSHALL takes a look. Yes, the light is on. Without comment, MARSHALL goes back to his reading.)* Marshall? *(MARSHALL grunts.)* Don't you think we should do something?
MARSHALL. *(From behind his paper.)* What do you think we should do, Ned?
NED. Tell somebody? Notify somebody?
MARSHALL. *(Looking at NED around his reading.)* Who somebody, Ned?
NED. Uh—
MARSHALL. What are you gonna tell 'em, Ned?
NED. That the light's on.

*(At this, MARSHALL does put down his reading.)*

MARSHALL. You're going to tell somebody that the light's on.

NED. I thought we should.

MARSHALL. Because it's our job?

NED. Yeah. We're supposed to—

MARSHALL. We're supposed to use our judgment, Ned.

NED. The light's on, Marshall. Isn't it?

MARSHALL. You know it is, Ned.

NED. Then we're supposed to call.

MARSHALL. Simple as that. Ned, in all the time we've been here— How long have you been here, Ned?

NED. Almost fifteen years.

MARSHALL. Fifteen years. I've been here eighteen years, Ned. In all that time, have you ever seen the light go on?

NED. No.

MARSHALL. Not once?

NED. No.

MARSHALL. Not even a blink?

NED. No.

MARSHALL. Have you ever heard of the light going on?

NED. No.

MARSHALL. Not even once? Not one single time?

NED. No.

MARSHALL. OK.

NED. But—

MARSHALL. Now it's on.

NED. That's right.

MARSHALL. And what are you going to do? Are you going to come unglued, Ned? Lose your head? Go to pieces? All the training, all the trust that's been placed in you, and me, are you going to just toss that out the window and hit the panic button? Are you, Ned?

NED. *(Summoning his courage.)* I think we should call. *(MARSHALL shakes his head, disgusted. NED becomes agitated.)* Don't you? What do you think we should do, Marshall? Because the light is on. It's definitely on. It's—on.

MARSHALL. I can see the light, Ned.

NED. OK.

MARSHALL. The question, now that the light is on, is what do we do about it.

NED. OK.

MARSHALL. Now the fact that the light is on can mean, I think, as I run over the possibilities in my mind, one of two things. If you think of any other possibilities, Ned, just jump right in, OK?

NED. OK.

MARSHALL. Possibility Number One: The light is defective. Meaning: There is no crisis.

NED. Boy, I don't see how that's possible, Marshall.

MARSHALL. It's like in your car, Ned. Happened to me last month. I'm drivin' along, all of a sudden this light comes on: "Check engine." Oh Mamma, I thought my car was gonna blow up. I pulled over as fast as I could and called the dealer. Talked to a mechanic. "This light just came on!" Know what he did, Ned? He laughed! Said it happens all the time, sooner or later. Doesn't mean a thing. Nothin's wrong with the engine, the light's busted. All I hadda do was pull the fuse. No more light. Next time I take it in, they'll fix it. Car runs fine. Saved myself worry, aggravation, all that time, a couple hundred bucks. You see what I'm sayin'? Could be the same situation we got right here.

NED. How do you know that?

MARSHALL. We don't. I'm saying it's a possibility. Ned, I'm saying it should be checked before we turn weapons of mass destruction loose. Maybe we should check the bulb before we unleash Armageddon. Don't you think we should do that?

NED. I guess so. *(Pause.)* How do we check the light?

MARSHALL. I'm not sure.

NED. Marshall, this isn't like your car. Do you know how many fail-safe systems are supporting this light? They've got redundancy piled on redundancy, backups on the backups, all to make sure this light works. And now—now—

MARSHALL. In the first place, Ned, let me remind you: To err is human. OK?

NED. OK.

MARSHALL. Secondly, if humans can err, think about governments. Humans make mistakes. Governments are mistakes. Think about all those glorious hi-tech systems they've built to insure that this one crummy little light cannot fail. OK? Now I ask you: What have they done? They've just increased their chances for error, that's all. In fact, if you think about it, they've put so much work into this one light that they've practically guaranteed a screwup. It's inevitable. It's like any government system, Ned. It gets so big and complicated that it gets stupid. They ever make a mistake on your paycheck?

NED. Sure.

MARSHALL. Screw up your vacation time?

NED. Yeah.

MARSHAL. Spell your name wrong?

NED. *(Brightening.)* All the time.

MARSHALL. You see?

*(There is a euphoric pause while they reflect on this happy news. MARSHALL returns to his reading.)*

NED. Marshall? *(MARSHALL grunts.)* What is the second possibility?

MARSHALL. *(From behind reading.)* That the light isn't broken.

NED. *(Wetting his lips.)* And we're really under attack?

MARSHALL. That's right.

NED. My God.

MARSHALL. *(Comes out to face NED.)* Exactly.

NED. What?

MARSHALL. Prayer, Ned. A moment with your Maker. Forget about making a call. If that light is working, I suggest you get down on your knees.

NED. That's not in the manual.

MARSHALL. Screw the manual, Ned. If that light isn't broken—

NED. I know.

MARSHALL. What are we talking about? The sky dark with nuclear missiles? The lucky ones die in the blast. The survivors experience the effects of global radioactive contamination. Or maybe it's not bombs. Maybe it's biochem, anthrax, ricin, sarin—choose your poison, Ned.

NED. No.

MARSHALL. And what would happen if we did follow the book? Panic. And what kind of a response would we get? Chaos. Bickering over what to do. Interagency quarrels, interdepartmental breakdowns, isolated power grabs, all the top leaders heading for cover, in bunkers, leaving the rest of us to—

NED. Stop. No more.

MARSHALL. That's the second possibility, Ned. You asked me. You want estimates on the initial casualties?

NED. No.

MARSHALL. Fifty million, minimum. That's before retaliation, of course. Which comes as a direct result of our response to the light.

NED. *(A final desperate plea.)* Don't you think we should call?

*(There is a pause while they consider this. CASEY enters.)*

CASEY. Hey, guys.

MARSHALL. Casey. Look at this.

CASEY. *(Sees the light.)* Whoa.

MARSHALL. What do you think?

CASEY. Maybe it's broken.

MARSHALL. That's what I've been trying to tell him. He wants to call.

CASEY. Hoo, I don't know about that. You make that call—

MARSHALL. That's right.

CASEY. That's serious. You start a chain reaction—

MARSHALL. Yowza. Get the picture, Ned?

NED. But it's our job to notify them if the light goes on.

CASEY. No, it isn't.

NED. How do you figure?

CASEY. Look, if they wanted it like that, Ned, they'd make the whole system automatic. There'd be no delay whatsoever. Those circuits ever fire up, boom, we'd launch, automatic, instantaneous, everything we've got.

MARSHALL. We're here to prevent that.

NED. You're saying we do nothing? No matter what?

*(Pause.)*

CASEY. Say, I'm going out for sandwiches. You guys want anything?

MARSHALL. I'll have smoked turkey with mayo and onion.

CASEY. Lettuce on that?

MARSHALL. No.

CASEY. Bun?

MARSHALL. Kaiser.

NED. I don't believe you guys! The world—the whole world could be—

CASEY. You want a sandwich or not?

NED. *(Pauses, gives in.)* Hard salami, tomato, lettuce on whole wheat.

CASEY. Mayo?

NED. No, I'm trying to cut down.

CASEY. OK. I'll be back.

*(CASEY exits. MARSHALL goes back to his reading. NED stares at the light. NED gets on his knees and prays. Gets back in his chair, looking at the light. Begins to pick up and shuffle his cards. The light goes off. He doesn't see this, then notices it.)*

NED. Hey! Marshall!

*(MARSHALL grunts.)*

NED. Nothing.

*(NED resumes his game. The light begins to blink. NED jumps behind his chair, stares at it. To dark.)*

**THE END**

# MEOW

by

## Val Smith

## MEOW
### by Val Smith
Directed by Frank Deal

*Pat:* Stephanie Zimbalist
*Linda:* Peggity Price
*Waitress:* Sara Sommervold

Scenic Designer: Paul Owen
Costume Designer: Kevin R. McLeod
Lighting Designer: Greg Sullivan
Sound Designer: Mark Huang
Properties Designer: Mark Walston
Stage Managers: Heather Fields, Juliet Horn,
Charles M. Turner III
Dramaturgs: Megan Shultz, Amy Wegener

## CHARACTERS

PAT. Early forties. Married. Has a teenage daughter.
LINDA. Late late thirties. Divorced.
Both are attractive, intelligent middle-class women. Both are friends
and have worked in the same office for years.
WAITRESS. Early twenties. Attractive. Exudes 'tude.

## SETTING

A booth in a restaurant. The restaurant is a few blocks from the
office where both women work. It's the kind of place where office
workers congregate after hours to catch a drink before going home.
They don't stay for dinner because, let's face it, the food is bad.
The atmosphere is ferns and ceiling fans and quaint stuff on the
walls—in other words, a "manufactured" neighborhood bar feeling
which never for a minute fools anybody that the place isn't a
franchise.

## TIME

Friday. Two hours after work.

## MEOW

*(A table in a restaurant. At Rise, LINDA is nursing what's left of a vodka tonic. The WAITRESS has recited a long list of Specials with some difficulty.)*

WAITRESS. Finally *(Pause.)* there's our red snapper grilled in ... *(Pause.)* herbed butter and topped with peanut and ginger sauce served with ... *(Pause.)* special Jamaican-style gratin potatoes and the vegetable medley—

LINDA. —Jamaican-style—?

WAITRESS. —gratin potatoes. Yeah. *(Beat.)* They're potatoes that are kindahhh—

LINDA. —Gratinized?

WAITRESS. Yeah!

LINDA. So you haven't had them.

WAITRESS. Randy the busboy says they're really good. *(Beat.)* 'A course Randy'll eat anything.

LINDA. I'll just stick with a whiskey sour. And a Merlot for my friend.

WAITRESS. Done with the Happy Hour won-tons?

*(WAITRESS moves to take them.)*

LINDA. *(Moves to hang onto them.)* Nahhht quite! *(Pause.)* You know, these were so yummy, could we have another batch?

WAITRESS. 'Kay. *(Beat.)* So. You don't want dinner ...

*(PAT enters and sits down.)*

PAT. *(Overlapping.)* Maybe they've got some good specials ...

WAITRESS. Well ... *(Clears throat. Here we go again.)* ... there's our breast of chicken rolled in polenta ...

LINDA. *(Interrupting.)* Thanks, thank you! That won't be necessary ...

PAT. No?

LINDA. *(To PAT.)* Trust me. *(To WAITRESS.)* We're on a strict semi-liquid diet. *(Hands the WAITRESS the menus.)* But thanks. *(Pause.)* Oh, and don't forget ... *(The WAITRESS is gone.)* ... our drinks. I get the feeling that—like Shane—her work here is done. *(Beat.)* How's Dan?

PAT. Not home yet. Left another message. Gawd, poor dog is gonna be hopping from leg to leg. And from leg to leg.

LINDA. Dan usually work this late?

PAT. I keep tellin' him he's gotta negotiate something like normal hours. You're so lucky. You don't have a dog to feed, or a husband you have to check in with, or a teenage daughter you have to delude yourself is at her girlfriend's house baking cookies.

LINDA. Yeah. *(Beat.)* I'm so stoked we're gonna be working together on this investment retreat.

PAT. Hawaii! A *budget*!

LINDA. Are you kidding me?

PAT. They're giving *us* money! Can you believe it!

LINDA. Somebody must have died at main office.

PAT. Whoohooo! Look out! Yes!

PAT and LINDA. —Together again!

*(They laugh wickedly and clink glasses. A beat.)*

LINDA. Did I tell you? That damn Sheila broke the copier again.

PAT. She only uses the thing four times a year. She breaks it every single time. How is that possible?

LINDA. Oh, and she's refined her technique. Now she doesn't even have to touch it. Now all she has to do is stand by it. And I mean it *totally* breaks. Not a simple paper clog. Oh no. There you might have hope. Sheila breathes on it, call in the surgeons. Everybody has to trek downstairs with their stuff and take a number. Gawd, it's *such* a pisser. She approaches, I hear myself saying, "Sheila! Let *me* do that for you!"

PAT. Hmmm. Maybe it's a—tactic.

*(LINDA considers this.)*

LINDA. No. I don't think Sheila's smart enough for a—tactic.

PAT. *(Pause.)* Do you like Sheila?

LINDA. Do I like Sheila? *(Pause.)* Do I like Sheila. To be truthful, I don't think much about Sheila. Unless she wants to use the copy machine.

PAT. You know how some people just—rub your fur the wrong way. Sheila does that to me.

LINDA. Oh yeah? What's she do?

PAT. She doesn't have to *do* anything. She just bugs the hell out of me.

LINDA. Yeah. Yeah-h-h-h. Plus she's this big around.

*(LINDA touches her thumb and forefinger to indicate circumference.)*

PAT. You think that's it?

LINDA. Isn't it?

PAT. *(Pause.)* Is this what they call being retro?

LINDA. Oh yeah.

PAT. I don't know why Sheila pisses me off.

LINDA. Yes, you do. She's young and she's thin and she's a big doof. She breaks the copy machine.

PAT. Maybe she affects me like she does the copier. Maybe she gives off microscopically destructive vibrations.

LINDA. Just be thankful you don't have Beth Silver in your section. You want to talk somebody rubbing your fur the wrong way. Ughhhh.

PAT. What?

LINDA. What do you mean what? I told you about Beth Silver. The spandex mini-skirts. To here. You sit across from her at a meeting, you feel like her gynecologist. The guys love it.

PAT. I'll bet they do.

LINDA. No surprises there.

PAT. *(Beat.)* Are we bitter?

LINDA. My, we're in a philosophical mode tonight. Bitter. Naturally. But we have a right to be.

PAT. I always feel weird trashing other women.

LINDA. Yeah? Since when?

PAT. I don't even *know* Sheila—

LINDA. You don't have to *know* Sheila to know Sheila. There's nothing to know. *(Beat.)* And with Beth—Well, there you know more than you *want* to know. The woman is an anorexic, collagen-injected wench-bag. *(Pause.)* Got a kickin' fine stylist though.

PAT. Lin-dah.

LINDA. What? That's not catty. That's truthful.

PAT. *(Beat.)* I mean, what we're doing here is so much a sign of the disenfranchised, I can't tell you.

LINDA. Whoa-ho-ho!

PAT. I mean it. What are we actually doing here?

LINDA. We're dishing.

PAT. We're venting.

LINDA. Exactly.

PAT. Exactly! I mean, we could concentrate our attacks upwards, at the actual source of our anger. But what do we do? We funnel our frustrations down the pyramid. At those less powerful—women we barely know—or across the pyramid, at each other—

LINDA. I hate to ask this, Pat, but ... did you like, read a book or something?

PAT. I'm serious. I've been thinking about this a lot lately. For instance, take—ah—well, take my daughter. Joannie's drop-dead gorgeous—

LINDA. —She is—

PAT. —She's gorgeous—and smart, and sweet. And here I am. Approaching the middle of my life—

LINDA. —Wow. And I thought we were the same age—

PAT. —yes, the low, low, low end of our forties—and I am being made increasingly aware that I'm no longer the fresh young thing I once was. The figure's dumpy—

LINDA. No way!

PAT. Yes, Linda, way. No amount of exercise or dieting can stem this slow, relentless downward slide of decay.

*(Pause.)*

LINDA. Two words, Pat. *(Beat.)* Plastic. Surgery.

PAT. Now, see—why? Why should I keep some—some scalpel-wielding huckster in three-hundred dollar loafers and a cigar boat in Florida just because I want the illusion of turning back the clock? Why not just keep buying different mirrors? Or, or, better still, why isn't how I *actually* look good enough?

LINDA. Why?

PAT. Yes! Why?

LINDA. In four words? Beth. Silver. Gets. Promotions.

PAT. *(Beat.)* That is so—twisted!—That is so revoltingly—disgustingly—

LINDA. —Archaic Sexist Chauvinistic Crapola?

PAT. Yeah!

LINDA. And yet, ya know, so inescapably *there*.

PAT. Not to mention it's unfair to Beth Silver.

LINDA. Sorry. Something must have flown in my ear.

PAT. Well, how will Beth Silver ever know whether she got her upgrade because of her brain—or because of her skirt?

LINDA. A better question might be, does Beth Silver care? Have a won-ton before I hoover them all.

PAT. But, really, think about where all this leads, Linda. My own daughter, for god's sakes. My own daughter who is *fifteen* years old! Now, how is *she* competition?

LINDA. Kids that age can be real turds.

PAT. No! It's the culture! It's a culture wherein the second, as a woman, you turn forty, your stock plummets. Blammo. Off the board. Might as well be Brown-Williamson. No wonder we're all so insecure. And it isn't gonna change until we change it!

LINDA. Right on. I am woman. Hear me roar.

PAT. I have a husband who loves me—we've had our problems, who hasn't—I have a good job, I have a great kid, I have my health. So why waste energy tearing into other women who happen to be younger or thinner?

LINDA. Or both. *(The younger, thinner WAITRESS appears with a Merlot and a Manhattan. She puts the drinks down and starts off. LINDA takes a sip.)* WHOA THERE, FURY! *(The waitress returns.)* I didn't order this.

WAITRESS. *(Pause.)* 'Kay. No prob.

LINDA. I *hate Manhattans. That's* a Manhattan.

*(The WAITRESS picks the drink up and sniffs it, puts it back down.)*

WAITRESS. Whadya order?

LINDA. I ordered a whiskey sour. And we were hoping for won-tons.

WAITRESS. 'Kay.

PAT. *(Jumping in.)* I understand. I used to waitress. You get busy—

WAITRESS. Oh tell me. Man, it's like E.R. back there—

PAT. —Really?

WAITRESS. —Flu. Yeah. I'm okay. But we got two servers out. The chef and the busboy are taking turns hurlin' in the bathroom—

LINDA. Okayyy! I hate to break up the Department of Health survey but might it be possible to get my whiskey sour? Forget the won-tons.

PAT. Linda.

WAITRESS. *(Long pause. Cool stare.)* 'Kay. No prob.

LINDA. You can take—

*(But WAITRESS exits without the Manhattan.)*

PAT. *(Beat as she notices LINDA's expression.)* What?

LINDA. "I used to be a waitress ... I understand ..." Pat. The woman has a wind tunnel where her brain should be.

PAT. Oh, and isn't it easy to pick on food service personnel?

LINDA. All I want is what I ordered. How does that make me a villain?!

PAT. *(Overlapping.)* She got the order a little scrambled doesn't mean she's a ditz. Harried perhaps. Ditz—not.

LINDA. Okay. *(Beat.)* If I complain to the manager, am I going up the pyramid?

PAT. Linda.

LINDA. If the manager is a woman, am I still going up the pyramid? Or am I going down the pyramid? Or am I really going across—

PAT. Linda!

LINDA. I just want to know—what's the book? "Running With—" what? Hamsters?!

PAT. Admit it, you're jealous of how she looks.

LINDA. What?! I am not! I'm complaining because she's lousy at her job!

PAT. Oh? Young and thin. And a ditz. *You* pointed it out.

LINDA. I don't believe this! Okay. Okay. *(Beat.)* Are you jealous of me?

PAT. What's that got to do with anything?

LINDA. You heard me.

PAT. No, I'm not jealous of you.

LINDA. How do you know this altercation that we are having is not just an excuse, a—a—way of disguising your own attack across the pyramid?

PAT. I'm not attacking you. You're my friend.

LINDA. And you've never been jealous of a friend? Never, ever?

PAT. *(Doubtful.)* No.

LINDA. Not even the time I got that bonus for processing the most—?

PAT. You earned it. I was happy for you!

LINDA. Never. Ever.

PAT. *(Beat.)* Well. Okay. Maybe. In the past.

LINDA. *(Great news.)* Really? When?

PAT. A few—isolated—moments. They were there. Then they were gone. I didn't feel good about them. Can't even remember them—

LINDA. Try.

*(A beat.)*

PAT. Christmas party at our house. Three years ago.

LINDA. Oh, yeah. *(Pause.)* Yeah?

PAT. You had on that green dress—

LINDA. Yeah. The one that made me look like I had cleavage. I loved that dress.

PAT. You looked nice.

*(A beat.)*

LINDA. That's it?

PAT. Yeah.

LINDA. Me in the green dress? That's it?

PAT. Dan said he thought you—he said you looked sexy.

LINDA. Oh. *(Pause.)* Dan said that.

PAT. Yeah.

LINDA. Oh. *(Pause.)* Well. *(Pause.)* Nice of him.

PAT. He was right. You did.

LINDA. Yeah, I did. *(A beat.)* You did too.

PAT. No, I didn't.

LINDA. Sure you did.

PAT. I didn't. You don't even remember what I was wearing.

LINDA. Um, wasn't it the gold number with the—sleeves—

PAT. No! I couldn't *fit* into that. I wore a tent made out of purple velvet.

LINDA. *(A bad memory.)* Oh, oh yeah.

PAT. Oh, who cares!

LINDA. Yeah, who cares! *(A beat.)* Wow. Christmas. Yeah. Boy, were we hammered that night. You passed out in the den. Wow. I'd almost forgotten. *(Laughs. A beat.)* So. Dan say anything else?

*(A beat.)*

PAT. Linda!

LINDA. What?

PAT. Geez! What else would Dan have to say? *(Beat.)* Linda? *(Beat.)* What else would Dan have to say?

*(A long moment. PAT stares at LINDA. LINDA shrugs, avoids PAT's gaze. Something has indeed happened in the past. How is she going to get out of this one? After a moment, PAT swats LINDA's arm.)*

LINDA. Ow! What?

PAT. You are so devious.

LINDA. Okay.

PAT. You had me buying it!

LINDA. Yeah?

PAT. You know you did—

LINDA. Oh, I know. Give me "up, down, across the pyramid." Geez, Pat, where do you come up with this stuff?

PAT. Just been on my mind. For awhile. *(Beat.)* Hey. I know how much you despise Manhattans but *(Picks up her glass to toast)*—?

LINDA. Sure. *(Raising her glass.)* To us.

PAT. To us. *(They clink glasses.)* Together again.

*(Lights go to Black.)*

**END OF PLAY**

# DAMAGES TO TONY

by

## Matthew Southworth

## DAMAGES TO TONY
### By Matthew Southworth

Directed by Sandra Grand
Dramaturg: Val Smith

*Julia:* Trina Fischer
*Leo:* Kyle B. Hamman

Scenic Designer: Tom Burch
Costume Designer: Joyce Drake
Lighting Designer: Paul Werner
Sound Designer: Mark Huang
Properties Designer: Mark Walston
Stage Manager: Jennifer Wills
Assistant Stage Managers: Patty Thoreson,
Laura Jean Wickman

## DAMAGES TO TONY

*(Hospital cafeteria. JULIA and LEO sit in folding chairs at the
narrow end of a table. Down the table someone has left a barely
eaten cherry Danish on a Styrofoam plate with a wadded napkin on it. JULIA pours Sprite from a can into cups in front of
each of them.)*

LEO. He's going to be okay.

JULIA. You're always so sure.

LEO. Tough day.

JULIA. I know it's been a tough day, Leo.

LEO. I know you're upset.

JULIA. He's the most important thing in the world to me.
*(Pause.)* The sound... made me sick.

LEO. I know. Don't think about it.

*(LEO reaches out to JULIA.)*

JULIA. I don't feel like being touched.

LEO. Julia, I didn't break his leg.

JULIA. I'm not gonna fight with you tonight.

LEO. I don't want to fight.

JULIA. Why weren't you watching him?

LEO. I was.

JULIA. I wasn't getting the food for five minutes. You can't
take care of him for five minutes?

LEO. Julia, it took a split-second, okay? Tony fell. I didn't push
him, he fell. Two-year-old kids fall all the time. You weren't so far
away anyway and you weren't watching him.

JULIA. Fine.

*(A pause.)*

125

LEO. Would you pour more into mine please?

JULIA. What?

LEO. The Sprite. Half and half.

JULIA. Jesus.

LEO. I'd buy my own if I could. *(Pause.)* It's going to really slow down potty training.

JULIA. Yes.

LEO. I was looking forward to that. I can't pay the car bill now.

JULIA. I know.

LEO. They'll take it.

JULIA. My head is killing me.

LEO. How're we gonna get around without a car? To work even. Give me your hand.

JULIA. Leo ... it'll go away.

LEO. Here.

JULIA. I hate this, you always do it too hard.

LEO. I won't do it too hard.

*(LEO takes her hand and massages the meaty part between her thumb and forefinger.)*

JULIA. We're in trouble, Leo. We already owe a fortune and now this.

LEO. We'll figure it out.

JULIA. No, we can't afford this. It's a total fucking scam. Insurance costs a fortune and it costs you a fortune to not have insurance.

LEO. We'll work it out, I promise.

JULIA. Do you know how much it costs to stay overnight? More than the Hilton, I'll tell you that. And they want us to bring him back every week.

LEO. It's not fair, I know. Poor little guy.

JULIA. He's never gonna be able to run well. His legs are already bowed, and obviously the other surgeries didn't make that much difference, and now he breaks his thigh bone slipping in *orange* juice at a shopping mall?

LEO. Ssshhh.

JULIA. No, don't shush me.

LEO. I agree with you. *(A pause. LEO continues massaging JULIA's hand.)* When I was a kid, *I* wasn't real athletic, but I hung out with all the cool sports kids. I wasn't fast or that strong, but I used to read car magazines all the time. So this way I became like the car expert of our bunch of kids, right? I'd go to the store with my mom and she'd do the groceries and I'd go straight to the magazine rack. There was *Popular Mechanics* and *CarToons*, this comic strip thing about cars that always had teeth and nostrils and *Autoweek* and *Hot Rod*, oh my god, *Hot Rod* was *the shit*. And if I'd been good, Mom would buy me one about once a month, I guess, and I'd read the magazine in the car on the way home and make myself sick to my stomach. Is your head getting better?

JULIA. Yes.

LEO. So I'd finish this magazine and start cutting it up and making this huge collage on my wall with all of these cars and choppers and trucks sometimes. And of course the bikini babes always draped over them. The guys would come over and we'd look at the collage and they'd ask me questions about the cars and try to stump me like "what kind of engine's this one got?" or "what colors did this one come in?" and I'd always get them. And we'd talk about what kind of car was better, what was faster, what one we'd get when we turned sixteen. Very important social decision. Most of those guys moved away or were hanging out with other people by high school, though. And you know, you turn sixteen and you're happy if you can afford a Pinto with 200,000 miles on it, never mind a Charger. You're paying with grass-cutting money, you know. I'd see people driving Chargers—they must've had rich parents—and who's riding in the passenger seat with 'em? Those bikini babes, just high school versions of 'em. Those were the guys who got really good jobs when they got out of high school.

JULIA. That's not because of the car.

LEO. I don't know, maybe, maybe not.

JULIA. I didn't get together with you because of your car.

LEO. And you're not a bikini babe.

*(JULIA takes her hand away. Pause.)*

JULIA. That guy didn't take two bites out of his Danish. That's a dollar sitting right there. Saying, "Eat me, spread some germs so you can go to the hospital and we can make more money."

LEO. So eat it.

JULIA. No way, did you see his skin?

LEO. I'm still thirsty. Wouldn't it be cool to have a Coke machine at your house? To give you cold Cokes all day if you wanted?

JULIA. Yeah, like those guys who have video games at home.

LEO. If you had a hundred billion dollars, what would you do?

JULIA. Buy things. Probably not a Coke machine.

LEO. Like what?

JULIA. I don't know. I'd probably go on a cruise. To Hawaii maybe. On The Love Boat. I'd wear my bikini.

LEO. Mm. What about me?

JULIA. Get your own one hundred billion. No, you could go. And Tony. We'd all get separate rooms. So we could lay all the things we bought for ourselves on the floor and look at them while we were getting into our swimsuits for the beach.

LEO. Then what?

JULIA. So then we'd go to the beach and all the people who live in Hawaii would be there and they'd be gold and shiny and we'd drink fruity drinks with our feet in the water and Tony'd play at the edge of the surf, trying to catch it. And I'd finish my drink and I'd get into the glittery silver bathing suit I would wear on that one day only and I'd walk him into the water with me while you sat on the beach, I don't know, talking to rich guys about the car you bought that day. Tony would giggle and I'd say, "Why are you giggling, Tony?" and he'd tell me that baby fish are nipping at his toes. And then he'd swim away, out into the ocean, towards the sun and I'd lay on my back and float. And the sky would be like a giant light blue bowl over the world with no clouds and I'd drift off, maybe even to sleep.

LEO. You'd drown.

JULIA. *(Enjoying her fantasy.)* Ssshhh. And when I'm asleep, maybe I'd dream about what things were like before I got my hundred billion dollars—that would be the best part, that I could remember not being able to afford anything. Everything would be black and white and cold as a cafeteria and Tony would swim up to me and spit water on me like a fountain and I'd wake up and see him in Technicolor. *(Pause.)* If I had a hundred billion dollars.

LEO. You'd be happy.

JULIA. I am happy. You grow up and drop unrealistic ideas and you act happy and one day you are.

LEO. I was watching him.

JULIA. I understand. You can't watch him every second.

LEO. But I was. He was playing in the plant and I told him not to. He was aggravating this guy and his wife sitting there drinking their orange juice. And Tony tried to run back to me but he couldn't balance very well and he kicked over the guy's juice on the floor. And he slipped. I watched the whole thing and I thought he just fell but his leg was twisted all under him in a funny shape. And he was crying and his pants were all wet with the juice.

JULIA. It was my fault, I should have taken him with me.

LEO. And the guy and his wife were more concerned with getting splashed, and they moved to the other end of the bench and acted like they didn't even see it happen. Like it wasn't that guy's fucking orange juice he slipped in.

JULIA. Let's not talk about it.

LEO. You don't set drinks on the ground, anyone knows that.

JULIA. Sshh.

LEO. No, not "sshhh." That's why they have those end table things, so that you have a place to put your drink so people won't knock it over.

JULIA. It was a mistake. We should have been paying closer attention.

LEO. It was an expensive goddamn mistake.

JULIA. Sshhh. There are other people in here.

LEO. It's his fault.

JULIA. He's just a kid, he doesn't know how to be careful yet.

LEO. The guy's fault. For leaving the juice down there. *(Pause.)* This is ridiculous. He's gonna pay for it. The whole thing.

JULIA. What?

LEO. The mental anguish.

JULIA. We can't do that. It was an accident.

LEO. But his. His accident.

JULIA. You can't just go and sue somebody because of an accident.

LEO. Yes, you can. You're *supposed* to.

JULIA. You know he didn't do it on purpose. Kids fall all the time.

LEO. But this time it was *our* kid. Julia, look. I love you. I want to make you happy again. In America, they don't let them get away with it. In America, even if you don't have jack shit, you can sue somebody. Julia—we can be happy again. Don't you want that? Don't you want to be happy?

*(Pause.)*

JULIA. I do. I want to be happy.


**END OF PLAY**

# THE INTERVENTION

by

## Anne Washburn

## THE INTERVENTION
### by Anne Washburn

Directed by: Sullivan Canaday White
Dramaturg: Ilana M. Brownstein

*Katy:* Andrea Whitley Clark
*Lu:* Alice Johnson
*Bret:* Tony Speciale
*Will:* Trip Hope
*Doug:* Cameron Carlisle
*Nina:* Catherine Ingman

Scenic Designer: Tom Burch
Costume Designer: Jessica Byrd Watters
Lighting Designers: Karen Hornberger, Matt Shuirr
Sound Designer: Jeremy Lee
Properties Designer: Craig Grigg
Stage Managers: John Armstrong, Catherine A. Kemp

### TIME
The Present.

### SETTING
A living room: A dumpy couch, a dumpy chair, a coffee table

### CHARACTERS (in order of appearance)
KATY
LU
BRET
WILL
DOUG
NINA

All are somewhere in their mid-to late-twenties.

*NOTE:* The play takes place in five scenes and is punctuated by swift blackouts, which indicate the passage of a small chunk of time.

Blackouts should be accompanied by an interesting blur of music and sound.

# THE INTERVENTION

## Scene 1

*(KATY, LU, BRET, and WILL.)*

KATY. She needs help. *That's* not the issue. But to lure her here, and confront her, and suddenly put it all out there: is this really the best way to deal with it?

LU. But what about that thing, That thing you read about or hear places, that thing where someone says, "That was the turning point for me; if that wouldn't have happened, very painful though it was, I would never have turned it all around." They say: I was very angry, at the time, *very* angry, but now I am very grateful.

KATY. Yes but that's what you say in retrospect. After it all works out. But what if it doesn't work out. *That's* the thing. Then you say: that was the turning point. That was the precise moment when my life turned into a horror movie.

LU. How can the Truth turn your life into a horror movie?

KATY. I thought it was *precisely* the Truth that turned your life into a horror movie.

BRET. It's like a war, okay? And you're in the trenches with the smoke rushing at you from the burning tank stalled 60 feet ahead of you on the battlefield, or they're knocking on your door late at night and you're lunging for the back window—or if you're just waking up in a cold sweat, fallen halfway out of bed, and you're pretty certain you dreamed the knock—but you're not *sure:* this is how you become someone. That's what I'm saying. This is how you form a character, or, an identity. You can't *become any-one* without a catalytic event. A national *or* personal catastrophe. Massive crisis. Lauren should count her lucky stars.

*(Pause.)*

LU. To begin with: they don't even *do* war like that anymore. Now it's all with computers.

KATY. Where is everyone?

WILL. What do we *say*? When she comes in?

BRET. We all shout: Surprise!

*(Blackout.)*

## Scene 2

*(DOUG and NINA burst in and stand for a moment, frozen with tension.)*

DOUG. Okay, we're not late.

NINA. We are late. Where's Lauren?

KATY. She's late.

NINA. I was like: *"Fuck.* We cannot be late." Do you think Lauren knows?

KATY. I think she's just late.

NINA. I can tell you, right off the bat, that this is way too casual a ... *(Searches for the word.)* tableau. If she comes in and sees this, and *then* everyone scrambles around and straightens up and looks concerned, she's not going to take this seriously.

DOUG. *(Lightly sarcastic.)* What do you want us to do—all line up facing the door?

LU. I think that would make her laugh.

WILL. That would scare *me* shitless.

BRET. I think the crucial thing is that no one blows this because these moments are so delicate. They hang by threads. We've all got to be preternaturally alert, really thinking, really focused, and just completely compassionate, just—everyone open your heart. All the way.

*(Pause.)*

NINA. Okay. Everyone do that. And while you're doing that— *(She gestures.)* Katy—I swear this'll work—on the sofa, with your hands folded on your lap, and Lu, if you are literally standing behind her *(Indicating KATY.)* and Doug, over there *(She indicates the chair to the side.)* so we can get some surround on this. Bret on the sofa. Will, on the sofa.

WILL. Hands in my lap?

NINA. No, on a guy that looks silly. Try crossing your arms.

*(He scrunches them against his body.)* Try crossing them in a relaxed manner. No. Try to look firm. But casual. But firm. Okay, we'll get back to you.

BRET. Nina, she's coming in that door at any moment. It's not going to matter what we look like if our mental attitude is completely unfocused.

KATY. I don't know that confrontation is the best way. Maybe we should try to change her from within.

DOUG. Should I look authoritative or should I move back into the shadows and look menacing?

LU. I feel like we should be saying "cheese."

NINA. Okay everyone just shut up. Let me look at you. *(She steps back. Looks at them. Starts to back towards the door.)* Okay, now I'm Lauren, coming into the room.

*(She exits. Knocks. Pause. Knocks again. WILL nudges KATY.)*

KATY. Oh! Come in.

*(NINA enters. Looks at everyone for a moment.)*

NINA. I don't feel at all moved, or, motivated by you guys. Bret's right. We have to focus. The mental attitude here sucks.

*(Blackout.)*

### Scene 3

*(BRET is sitting in the center of the couch staring intently at a cheapie tourist-quality voodoo doll. Everyone else is gathered around him on the couch.)*

WILL. This isn't the kind that comes with instructions. Some of them have the places all marked out where you're trying to put the pins in. Where do we put the pins in?

KATY. Do we need special pins?

NINA. Does anyone *have* pins?

*(Pause.)*

DOUG. We could just pinch it.

NINA. But where. Heart? Brain?

DOUG. Um, is it supposed to work ... are we supposed to be working on it like a machine, or, symbolically?

WILL. You can't just stick pins into it. You have to have a ceremony. I saw a ceremony at the voodoo museum in New Orleans but halfway into it the two guides got into a tussle for hegemony of the exhibit and the fake chicken was crushed and we all snuck out the back way. So I didn't see all of it. Not that they show you the real ceremony anyway. They keep parts back. The important parts.

LU. Okay, no. This isn't about any ceremony or system. This is about the power of raw belief.

DOUG. Well I respect that but in fact, practically, there's no way I'm believing without some kind of rigamarole. There is no express elevator out of Western Consciousness for me; if you're going to take me away you've got to take me by the stairs.

KATY. Oh alright. *(KATY stands up.)* I've got some pins somewhere ...

*(KATY starts to head off stage.)*

BRET. *(Looking up.)* Someone turn down the lights.

*(Instant blackout.)*

## Scene 4

*(In a blackout.)*

WILL. If we were Bodysnatchers, all we'd have to do would be to wait for her to fall asleep—*which is inevitable*—and then we'd just position a Pod by her sleeping body. And then we could sit back and relax.

*(Pause.)*

NINA. *What?*

WILL. Don't you ever do that? When I'm watching horror movies, and I'm getting really stressed out, I just think: well why am I identifying with the humans? Why don't I just identify with the powerful alien entities? And I do. And then the movie is really enjoyable. Unless the humans win in the end. But then I just think to myself: *Earthling propaganda.*

*(Pause.)*

NINA. *WHAT?*
BRET. Will, shut up. I'm trying to concentrate.
WILL. Right. Okay.

### Scene 5

*(The Lights are low. Everyone is sitting on the floor around the coffee table. BRET is in the middle, and he holds the doll upright. He pivots it, slightly, so that it appears to look at each member of the circle. They are, on the whole, hushed and expectant.)*

BRET. Say hello to Lauren everyone.
LU. *(Solemnly.)* Hello Lauren.
NINA. *(Crisply.)* Hello Lauren.
WILL. Hello Lauren.

*(KATY reaches out to touch the doll's hand with her fingertip.)*

KATY. Hello Lauren.

*(Pause. The doll "waits.")*

DOUG. *(Terse.)* Hi. *(Pause. A few glances are exchanged.)* Well? Is she going to do anything? Or are we supposed to do something?
BRET. She's suspicious.
NINA. Katy, do you want to start this off?
KATY. Um ...
BRET. We're going to have to restrain her.
KATY. Physically?
BRET. She's figured out what's up and she's turning to go.
KATY. Okay, well—

*(BRET presses the doll flat into the table.)*

BRET. Okay, you can talk now.
DOUG. Is this necessary?
BRET. If you walked into this room would *you* stay?

*(Pause. They stare at the doll.)*

KATY. *(Intent.)* Lauren. I know this is all a shock. I know that this seems like we're ganging up on you and it seems like a betrayal but believe me, this wasn't easy.

LU. No.

KATY. *(Sticking the doll with a pin thoughtfully.)* It would have been far easier to let you go on with your life and to let you go. We wouldn't do this if we didn't love you, and this isn't about what's *wrong* with you. This is about all of the ways in which you aren't *you* anymore.

LU. This is about reaching into you and pulling you *out* of yourself. Before you *really* become a different person. Bret, can I? *(She carefully transfers the doll from BRET's grasp and holds it to her chest, clutching it tightly as though it might spring away. LU, sticking the doll with a pin as KATY did.)* Sweetie, I know it's been rough. I know it's been rough. But you're wrong to believe that because you've lived your life more intensely, you've lived it more deeply. You're wrong to think that we can't understand you anymore, and that we have no idea what you're going through and that we have no *insight* on your life. You're wrong to think that we can't help you. Because we can. And you have to let us. You have to.

DOUG. *(Impulsively.)* Lu, give me Lauren.

*(LU passes the doll to BRET who passes it to DOUG.)*

BRET. Hold on tight, 'cause she's pissed.

DOUG. *(Reluctantly sticking a pin in—either right at the start, or at the end.)* It's like... what Katy said. As though there's a *thing* in you that's gone wrong, a bad object, lodged inside you. And I wish that I could just shake it out of you, that I could cut you open and pull it out and sew you up again, and you'd be fine. And now I know why they used to—to get demons out of people—why they used to do those horrible things to them; I'd like to punish you— not for anything you've done to me because we're not that close— but I watch the way you treat yourself and I think: she shouldn't be allowed to get away with that. And I've never said this to another human being but I think you should bow down and pray. And I'm an agnostic. *(He pauses. WILL reaches out.)* Wait just a sec'. I'm not sure I'm done yet.

WILL. I just remembered something and I know exactly what I want to say. And if I don't say it right now I'll forget it.

DOUG. Okay.

*(They transfer the doll. When it is in his grasp, WILL turns away and huddles over it, whispering inaudibly into its ear. He sticks it with lots and lots of pins, very insistently and methodically.)*

NINA. Will, what are you doing?

WILL. This is private.

DOUG. I thought what *I* said was pretty private. But I said it in public.

LU. Will, this is supposed to be—

NINA. There's a group dynamic we're trying to maintain here.

WILL. Almost done.

LU. *(With a facial expression.)* Well. Whatcha gonna do.

*(WILL turns around and flings the doll violently onto the center of the table.)*

DOUG. *Jesus*, Will.

*(KATY and BRET dive for the doll at the same time. BRET grabs it first and holds it upright on the table, as at the beginning of the scene.)*

KATY. Is she okay?

NINA. Will that's completely uncool.

BRET. *(Neutral.)* She's mad.

WILL. Good.

BRET. No, I mean she's really mad.

WILL. Good. She's mad, I'm mad.

*(BRET starts to move the doll towards WILL, doll-step by doll-step.)*

BRET. She's coming towards you, Will.

WILL. Forget it, Bret.

BRET. She's coming closer. And closer. And closer.

*(There is a knock on the outside door. NINA and KATY shriek, DOUG yelps. Everyone turns to face the door, frozen.)*

WILL. Oh my God! Don't let her in!

*(Blackout.)*


**END OF PLAY**

# LET THE BIG DOG EAT

by

## Elizabeth Wong

## LET THE BIG DOG EAT
### by Elizabeth Wong
Directed by Frank Deal

*Ted:* William McNulty
*Bill:* Brian Keeler
*Michael:* Fred Major
*Warren:* William Cain

Scenic Designer: Paul Owen
Costume Designer: Kevin R. McLeod
Lighting Designer: Greg Sullivan
Sound Designer: Mark Huang
Properties Designer: Mark Walston
Stage Managers: Heather Fields, Juliet Horn,
Charles M. Turner III
Dramaturgs: Meghan Davis, Michael Bigelow Dixon

## CHARACTERS
TED
BILL
MICHAEL
WARREN
(Ages 40 to 70)
## PLACE
A prestigious golf course. At the first tee.
## TIME
The Present.

PLAYWRIGHT'S NOTE: The men are avid golfers. They are impeccably at-
tired in tasteful clothes befitting their status. They take their golf game seriously.
Golf is precision.

Hierarchy, competition, alliance, and realignment of power and position are a
necessary part of the play's subtextual infrastructure, and need to be reflected by
actors, spatially. Golf is stillness.

The play is neither a cartoon, nor a caricature, but a fun fraternity—full of
good-natured teasing, roughhousing, and school-boy antics. But make no mistake—
they are powerful, confident, deferring to none, including each other.

In the Actors Theatre of Louisville production, the play began with a "rain
shower" of over-sized money of various denominations, floating onto the playing
area, augmented by a subtle green strobe, to a sound mix of cash registers and the
song, "For The Love of Money" by the O'Jay. This special effect worked sub-
limely as the golf course.

# LET THE BIG DOG EAT

*(A golf course. At the first hole. WARREN and MICHAEL, BILL and TED—four captains of industry at play, about to tee off. They are relaxed, convivial, fraternal.)*

BILL. *(To TED.)* Geez, that's kinda hard-core, Ted. We cannot be *the* lousiest golfers in the Fortune 500.

TED. We suck. In God we trust, and in golf we suck. That's why I'm taking up flyfishin', and you are taking the honor. After you, my friend.

BILL. No way, I really suck.

WARREN. *(To MICHAEL.)* The Shark handed me his driver, I swing, I hear a whoosh, I look up. I don't see it. That's because the ball is four inches from my left foot. In front of Greg Norman, I dinked! Twice! It was so humiliating. Dink!

MICHAEL. You wanna talk humiliation. I'm at the shotgun start of my own tournament on my own network, I whiff. From coast to coast in living color, from Epcot to Anaheim. Whiff. The sound of empty air. That's embarrassment!

TED. *(Interrupting.)* Hell Mikey, that's nothing. I was at Kapalua with Arnie and Jack, couldn't hit it past the goddamned ladies tees, and those guys invoked the goddamned rule. Had to play the rest of the hole with my dick hanging o.u.t.

*(BILL emits a loud raspberry.)*

MICHAEL. That's it. I declare a winner. Show us your big swing, Ted. We've already seen your big wallet!

BILL. First on the first tee, and first in charit-TEE!!!

WARREN. You win Ted! Let the big dog eat!

BILL/MICHAEL/WARREN. Chomp! Chomp!/Arrrooooo!/ Woof woof!

TED. Now, that's just it. I'm sick of being just a big growling stomach. A gigantic digestive tract, with dollars dripping from my maw. Chomp chomp chomp. Hell, I'm no poorer than I was nine months ago, and the world is maybe a lot better off. *(Beat.)* Okay, all right, what do you say, we play a penny per hole, greenies get a nickel, par gets a dime. High score buys a round of milk at the 19th.

BILL. Whew! For a minute there, I thought I'd have to pledge a billion to the Red Cross just to play this round.

TED. Okay! Now you're talkin'.

WARREN. Don't worry Bill, I'll spot you. Better yet, I'll take back a few million shares of Cap Cities, if Mike here doesn't mind. That should make a nice, sizable contribution to the Mickey Mouse Fan Club.

MICHAEL. Come on Ted, face it, you turned us into measly cheapskates. Bill here gave some $135 million away last year, and now it sounds like chump change. Hell, you're making us all look bad. Right Warren?

TED. Redeem your immortal soul! Now, one of you slackers tee up!

WARREN. Well, Mike, I know how you can redeem your *immoral* soul. Sell off your hockey team. Disperse the funds in ten-year increments, $100,000 per annum to Greenpeace or Save The Rain Forest.

MICHAEL. Not my team! I love my team. Ted got to keep his team. I'll sell off the Magic Kingdom first.

BILL. Oh nooooo! Not Mickey! Don't liquidate Mickey!

WARREN. Next thing you know, Mickey and Minnie will be living out of a cardboard box, sellin' shares of Disney in front of Mr. Toad's Wild Ride.

BILL/MICHAEL/WARREN. *(Harmonizing beautifully.)* M.O.U.S.Eeeeeeeeeeeee ... for sale!

TED. Hell, that sounds all right. Let's pass a law! Lobby! Make *that* the goddamn national anthem.

MICHAEL. Now that's a good idea. I'll have my people get some people to hire some people to work on that.

WARREN. Gentlemen, nothing wrong with a little strategic philanthropy, few things lubricate power faster than a well-placed seven-figure check to the right hospital or university.

TED. That's right, T-bone. Turn over a few shares of Time Warner every year, I feel good about that. Nothing wrong with working for a more humane world

BILL. *(To WARREN.)* But Brother T-bone, Brother Ted has fallen from the pure of faith. He no longer takes joy, as we do, in the pleasure of sheer accumulation. *(To TED.)* Blasphemer!

TED. Sure it's fun making money, watchin' it grow. Making so much, you never have to write a check or carry cash in your wallet. So many damned zeros and commas to make your mamma proud.

WARREN/BILL/MICHAEL. Amen./I heard dat./*Watch it grow!*

TED. Sure, money is a measure of success. I won't deny that, heck, we all have lived by its dipstick.

WARREN/BILL/MICHAEL. Whoever has the most! *Biggest dip wins!* That's right, uh huh!/Winner take all.

TED. But boys, I'm upping the ante. I'm playing a new game, with a new scorecard. Who's in with me? It's not how much you make, but how much you can give, give, give.

WARREN. Bill ...

BILL. Yup.

WARREN. I think Ted not only wants to top the Forbes' 400 list, but he wants to be tops on the list in that *American Benefactor* magazine too. We all know how photogenic you are Ted, and you too Michael.

MICHAEL. Thank you Warren, you are so kind. True, I'm happier donating to my own foundation since most non-profits are lousy with money management and ... it gives my wife something to ...

BILL. *(Interrupting.)* Move over George Soros! George is running scared, Skipper! The Ted wants to run with the big dogs— Feeney, Getty, Annenberg, Carnegie, Rockefeller. *(BILL runs in place.)* You know, Ted, when Warren isn't eating steaks, he's a real shark at bridge. King of the trump. He's so addicted, in one night, I bet he could win a billion easy.

TED. A billion *is* a nice round number.

WARREN. *(Raising right hand.)* I pledge to donate all my winnings to ... Gamblers Anonymous.

BILL. Ohmigosh T-bone, you have to give up cigars! The money you spend on Cohibas you could finance a small war.

WARREN. But I love my Cohibas. I can't give 'em up. Don't make me. They are so delicate.

MICHAEL. Well Warren, you could roll your own. I've been rolling my own since ...

BILL. *(Interrupting.)* Mikey, you spoiled my surprise. Tee, I bought you this old wooden cigar thing from Cuba, been in Castro's family for years. But ssssshhh. Don't tell Ted. Or he'll make me take it back, and donate the money to the *(Pointedly.)* American Lung Association.

TED. If you boys are through. We got 382 yards from the black to the pin. And we're burning daylight.

MICHAEL. I was saying, my buddy Schwartzenegger got me into packin' and rollin' my own stogies. Okay, I admit the first few I rolled were a bit bumpy and lumpy ...

TED. *(Interrupting.)* Dopey, Sleepy, Bumpy, Lumpy! Sounds like the goddamned seven dwarfs. Hell, maybe some of those good ol' boys want to play some goddamned golf!

WARREN. Now, gentlemen, the dwarfs are a pivotal variable. Huge valuation disparity relative to the market. Balance sheets haven't looked better in thirty years, they are awash in cash flow. Maybe the dwarfs should turn over their stock outright, claim 30% of their adjusted gross income in deductions. Avoid capital gains on any increases in value. Of course, Ted knows all about those juicy tax deductions, right Skipper?

TED. Tax nothing! It's a third of my net worth! This is going to cost me!

BILL. Nah, I see your game, old boy. You give it to the UN and the UN lets you broadcast TBS, CNN and the Atlanta Brave home games to the nice people of Timbuktu! Rumor has it, he may also buy out Barry, and send 'em The Home Shopping Network, you sly dog!!! Arrrroo!

MICHAEL. Not at all, gentlemen, I heard through very reliable sources, the poor man had to get his wife off his back! Jane wanted him to help her open up an acting school in Hanoi and a health club in Ho Chi Minh City!

*(They congratulate MIKE, with pats on the back and handshakes. MIKE beams.)*

BILL/WARREN. You win that one, Michael! Arrrrooo!/Good one, Michael! Let the big dog eat! Arrrrooooo!

TED. It's about compassion, boys. I gotta believe when you give from your heart, you got yourself a win/win situation.

MICHAEL. Speaking of heart, what about you, Bill? Not everyday we have a tri-zillionaire among us. Ready for that win/win scenario? When are you gonna ante up? Ted's waiting for you to fold, call, or raise.

BILL. Well Michael, I was thinking about that. Gee whiz, well, I could sell my house, it's worth about $40 million, but then my wife would really be mad at me.

MICHAEL. It's a good thing, Bill, you added that trampoline before The Ted here put us all on the hot seat.

WARREN. A man's castle isn't complete without his trampoline room.

BILL. Hey, it's great. I'm serious, you all should try it. It's really a good workout! I like to bounce. *(BILL bounces!)* Helps me think when I'm bouncing. I got the idea to start up MSNBC with a front-twisting somersault and landing on my butt. It's fun! Maybe when I'm bouncing, I'll think of a way to trump The Ted. Outdoing a billion-dollar giveaway takes some considerable bouncing.

TED. Well boys, maybe y'all should bounce on it. *(TED bounces, leads all in a lively bounce fest.)* Belly up to a man's game. Stop playing that tired two-dollar table. Shake loose something more than measly pocket change.

MICHAEL. *(Coyly.)* By God, I think he's right. Compared to you guys, all I got is pocket change. I'm just a lowly billionaire in waiting. Boo Hoo.

*(MICHAEL cries.)*

WARREN. There. There. You are catching up fast, that's what counts. But you better hurry it up, because the future makes me feel like an over-sexed guy in a whorehouse. The future is ripe for making more money. It's like this beautiful green manicured golf course. The fairway of opportunity, lots of hazards, but we know where they all are, and when we hit the green, we drain that bad boy for a million, ten million! My boy, the future is bright.

MICHAEL. The future is bright.

BILL. And ripe.

TED. It sure is.

*(All look dreamily down the fairway, relishing the idea of a lucrative future.)*

BILL. *(Gently.)* You know Ted, it's not like we don't give. We give. Right Michael?

MICHAEL. That's right. And Warren is going to be the biggest of the big-time givers. *Beyond* big. Don't be modest, Warren. Some $21 billion, after you-know-what happens, croak city, then *BAM,* everybody wins. Everybody goes to the bank.

BILL. It's cosmic the amount he'll leave behind. Beyond cosmic!

TED. *After,* Warren? But then you'll be dead. Give a billion right now, T-bone, you can make it back, then give a billion more. Enjoy the smile on some poor kid's face. Hell, put a thousand smiles on a thousand faces. You can't get that kind of pleasure from *worms,* six feet under.

BILL. Warren and I talked long about this. Even my kids won't get a big piece. I want them to understand the value of hard work. Make their own opportunities. I'm giving it all away, *after.*

WARREN. Right! You could say, we are working and saving for the future. It's a long-term thing, that's how we are doing it. Not before, *AFTER*.

BILL. After.

TED. Boys, what we got here is a dogleg right, with the green trapped left. Best line is straight out from the tee. There is our future, boys. Who's it gonna be? *(All back away from tee mound.)* This is gonna sound crazy. But Warrren, I had this dream. It was like that movie *Road Warrior.* Chaos everywhere. Everybody starving. People resorted to cannibalism. I think about that all the time. People eating each other to survive. Chomp chomp. It was terrible. The worst-case scenario. But I refuse to be cannibal. I would rather starve.

BILL. A billion dollars to feed the pigeons!

TED. I refuse to eat my fellow human beings. I would rather starve to death than be a cannibal...

BILL. A billion dollars to feed the ducks!

MICHAEL. A billion for the battle of the bulge! A billion for the war on pimples! Come on Warren, it's fun!

*(WARREN waves him off. He keeps his eyes on TED.)*

BILL. A billion to feed the hungry.
TED. Exactly.
MICHAEL. A billion to heal the sick.
TED. Exactly.
WARREN. Ted, you are so full of shit.

*(TED's next speech\*\* overlaps with the following chant by BILL, MICHAEL and WARREN.)*

BILL/MICHAEL/WARREN. *(One-upping each other.)*
A billion to house the homeless.
A billion to shelter refugees.
A billion.
A billion to educate children.
A billion for a cure for AIDS.
A billion for a cure for cancer.
A billion for human treatment of animals.
A billion to teach people to read.
A billion for national health care.
One billion.
A billion to end suffering.
A billion to end pain.

A billion for peace.

A billion to spread *luvvvv.*

TED. ** Very funny. Who's gonna tee off first? Warren? Bill? Michael? Okay, all right, you had your fun. You guys are doing this because you don't want to go first. Cowards. I'm onto your game. You'll do anything as long as some other sucker tees off first. Cowards! Pansies! We came to play some golf. I'm onto your game. Let's play. Let's go! You selfish bastards! *(BILL, MICHAEL and WARREN have ended their chant, and TED continues.)* Move aside. I'll show y'all how it's done again! Here it is—for a penny! Goddammit!

*(TED swings his driver. Whoosh. He freezes at the end of his follow-through. Blackout.)*

**END OF PLAY**

# WHAT ARE YOU AFRAID OF?

## A CAR PLAY

by

**Richard Dresser**

# A CAR PLAY

"Theater does not have to exist within the frame of buying a ticket to a two-hour event," explains Actors Theatre of Louisville Producing Director Jon Jory. "We have to seek other venues, forms and time limits to remain part of the contemporary lifestyle."

In the 1999 Humana Festival, one such experiment with venue, form and time was provided by Richard Dresser's *What Are You Afraid Of?*, a dramatic text that explores some possibilities of the Car Play. In this version of on-site theatre, audience members sit in the back seat of an automobile and watch the play performed by actors in the front seat. The familiarity of the setting evokes thoughts of voyeurism, déjà vu and audience participation. As Judith Newmark of *The St. Louis Post-Dispatch* explains, "The play challenges ingrained assumptions about what constitutes theater and about the audience's role in shaping it. Do we just sit back and say, 'Entertain me,' or can we alter the experience if we are more involved intellectually, emotionally, or, in this case, physically?"

*What Are You Afraid Of?* was presented at fifteen-minute intervals for several hours at a stretch by two different casts. The "set" was an old Lincoln Town Car parked outside the Actors Theatre of Louisville lobby—the car never left the curb. To enhance the play's expressionistic style, Dresser chose musical selections that were controlled by actors on the car's audio system. According to Dresser, "The limitations turned out to give the play its shape ... [I had to] strip away everything that is not essential. Not an extra word, not an extra syllable."

*—Sara Skolnick*

## WHAT ARE YOU AFRAID OF?
### by Richard Dresser

THE CAST
Directed by Stuart Carden
*Man:* Tudor Sherrard
*Woman:* Jessica Jory

THE CAST
Directed by Frazier W. Marsh
*Man:* Trip Hope
*Woman:* Ginna Hoben

Costume Designer: Kevin McLeod
Sound Designer: Malcolm Nicholls
Properties Designer: Ben Hohman
Dramaturg: Adrien-Alice Hansel

*(NOTE: The play is to be performed in a parked car. The two actors are in the front seat, the audience is in the back seat.)*

# WHAT ARE YOU AFRAID OF?

*(A MAN is driving by himself, grooving to the radio: "Sweet Hitch-hiker" by Creedence Clearwater Revival\*. He stops the car, leans over, opens the door.)*

MAN. *(To himself.)* Yes! There is a God!

*(A WOMAN gets in the car.)*

WOMAN. Thanks. I thought I was going to be out there by myself forever.

MAN. *(Checking her out.)* You? I don't think so.

WOMAN. Most people are such jerks, trapped inside their own personal heads. They never even see me.

MAN. I don't usually pick up hitchhikers. You're actually my very first. Aren't you afraid?

WOMAN. Of what?

MAN. Getting in a strange car. I could be anyone. I could be your absolute worst nightmare.

WOMAN. And I could be yours. *(A quick impression of a deranged lunatic.)* But you gotta take some risks sometime if you're gonna have a life, don't you?

*(As their eyes meet, the music changes: "Don't Worry Baby" by the Beach Boys\*. The car is stopped. He puts his arm around her.)*

MAN. Beautiful, isn't it?

WOMAN. Oh, you like toxic waste facilities?

MAN. No, you and me. Together. Can I kiss you?

WOMAN. I didn't think you brought me out here for the view.

MAN. I brought you here so we could be alone.

WOMAN. I guess all those "Danger" signs really do keep people away.

*(He kisses her. She pulls away.)*

MAN. That bad?

WOMAN. No, I just swallowed my gum.

MAN. Bummer. I'll spring for another piece later on. *(He kisses her again. She stops.) What?*

WOMAN. In a *car?*

MAN. C'mon, it's just the two of us. There isn't another soul for miles. Nobody ever needs to know.

WOMAN. It's just a little ... uncomfortable.

MAN. I've got an idea.

WOMAN. I bet you do.

MAN. Let's hop in back. The seat folds down. It'd be like a night at the Ritz.

WOMAN. Just kiss me.

*(He kisses her. They slide down on the front seat, out of sight. A blouse flies into the back seat. Then a brassiere. They come up to a seated position. They both sigh.)*

MAN. Wow.

WOMAN. My feelings exactly.

MAN. You're just ... well, I've never ... I mean ...

WOMAN. What *do* you mean?

MAN. To be honest. I think I'm in ...

WOMAN. What?

MAN. *(Struggles to say it.)* Lllll.... As you've probably guessed, I have ...

WOMAN. *What* do you have?

MAN. Strong feelings. Directed at you.

WOMAN. Gee.

MAN. You know what I mean.

WOMAN. Why can't you just say it?

MAN. Why do I need to say it if you know what I mean?

WOMAN. *(Teasing.)* C'mon, it's just the two of us. There isn't another soul for miles. No one ever needs to know.

MAN. It isn't that.

WOMAN. Then what?

MAN. I can say it.

WOMAN. When?
MAN. Soon. Don't rush me.

*(Pause.)*

WOMAN. Tonight? This week? This year? I'm just trying to get a rough idea.
MAN. Hey, relax! I'm going to say it!

*(Pause.)*

WOMAN. What are you afraid of?

*(As their eyes meet we hear a tape of the homicide-inducing "Barney" song: "I love you, you love me, we're a happy family..." \*)*

MAN. *(To the back seat.)* Would you kids shut up!
WOMAN. Please, honey, they've been in the car a *long time.* We've *all* been in the car a long time. *(To the back seat, sweetly maternal.)* Let's button our lips and throw away the key. Daddy's a little grouchy today.
MAN. Daddy isn't grouchy! Daddy's about to snap! Now what were those orders again?
WOMAN. *(Super-fast.)* Three Hamburger Happy Meals, two small cherry cokes, a large chocolate milk, I'll have Chicken McNuggets, medium fries, a super-size half-decaf coffee with sweet 'n' low, don't forget to ask for straws and extra ketchup ... and what do *you* want?
MAN. *(Aside.)* I want to kill myself. Then I want to kill Barney. *(He rolls down the window. Distorted Electronic Gibberish from a speaker. Continuing, to speaker.)* Excuse me?
WOMAN. Just tell him or her your order, honey. There are only about a billion cars behind us.

*(Electronic Gibberish.)*

MAN. Right. Okay. Three kiddie meals—
WOMAN. *(Calling toward speaker.)* Happy Meals!
MAN. Some drinks ...

---

\*Permission to perform the play does not indicate permission to use the song and that such permission must be obtained from the owners of the respective song.

WOMAN. *(Calling toward speaker, super-fast.)* Two small cherry cokes, one large chocolate milk, one super-size half-decaf with sweet 'n' low—

MAN. She wants a chicken sandwich—

WOMAN. *(Calls toward speaker.)* McNuggets!

*(Electronic Gibberish.)*

MAN. *(To the speaker.)* Right back at ya!

WOMAN. You forgot to get something for yourself.

MAN. It's okay. I couldn't keep anything down with Barney around. *(Suddenly wheels around to back seat.)* Okay, who threw that?

WOMAN. Sweetie? You're supposed to pull up to the window and get our food.

MAN. *(Glaring at each person in the back seat.)* We're not moving till one of you tells me who did it! Who looks guilty?

WOMAN. *(Looks at people in back.)* If you ask me they *all* look guilty.

MAN. Then they're all gonna pay!

WOMAN. I'm sure it was an accident, dearest.

MAN. It hit me in the back of the head! It could have put my eye out!

WOMAN. Would you *please* pull forward and get our food?

MAN. *(Staring straight ahead, tense.)* I'm trying.

WOMAN. Is the car *supposed* to be making that sound?

MAN. No. It isn't.

WOMAN. *(Looking in the back of car.)* Uh-oh. That black smoke isn't a good sign, is it?

MAN. Probably not, darling.

WOMAN. Oh, dear. What does it mean?

MAN. It means we can't go. We're stopped.

WOMAN. We can't be "stopped." We're blocking about a mile of traffic and we don't even have our food!

MAN. *(Suddenly wheels around to the back seat.)* Who said that? This is your last warning! Next time we get out of the car, I take off my belt, and God help us all!

WOMAN. Honey? Shouldn't you get help?

MAN. I do not need "help." I need a vacation!

WOMAN. We're *on* a vacation, remember? I meant for the car.

MAN. Help for the *car*? Are you insane? What, you think I'm going to go up to another guy and ask for *help*?

WOMAN. Why not? What are you afraid of?

*(As their eyes meet the song changes back to "Sweet Hitchhiker*."
The MAN and WOMAN are alone in the car, cruising along.)*

MAN. So where exactly are you going?
WOMAN. I don't know.
MAN. How can you not know where you're going?
WOMAN. How can you *know* where you're going?
MAN. Look, if you don't have any particular destination ...
WOMAN. Yes?
MAN. Well, I could take you ... anywhere.
WOMAN. Where do you *want* to take me?
MAN. I don't know. Wherever you want.
WOMAN. *(Disappointed.)* Oh. Well. There's an on-ramp to the
Interstate. I bet I could get another ride there.

*(The car stops. WOMAN opens the door.)*

MAN. Hey, I never even got your name.
WOMAN. All you had to do was ask.

*(WOMAN gets out of the car.)*

MAN. *(Desperate.)* There are so many things I want to tell you!
It seemed like there was really something between us. *(Thinks.)*
But we were having such a nice time I didn't want to spoil it if you
weren't interested and maybe once we got to know each other we'd
find out we didn't have much in common and maybe we'd even
grow to hate each other and this way, well, at least we both have a
nice memory, right?
WOMAN. What are you afraid of?
MAN. Me? Nothing!
WOMAN. Okay. Well, thanks for the ride!

*(WOMAN closes the door. She's gone.)*

MAN. *(To himself.)* Everything.

*(The MAN continues on his way, alone.)*

## END OF PLAY

# LIFE UNDER 30

**Eight ten-minute plays
about people under thirty
at the end of the 20th century.**

## LIFE UNDER THIRTY

*Life Under 30* is the umbrella title for eight ten-minute plays which premiered during the 1999 Humana Festival of New American Plays. Selected by Jon Jory—with input from ATL's literary staff that included, at the time, three persons under the age of thirty—these works introduce eight talented young playwrights to an international audience. Finding a venue to showcase young playwrights, as well as young actors and directors, was a major part of this year's Humana Festival. "From the quality of their work," wrote critic Dick Kerekes, "I realized and am pleased to announce that the future of the theatre seems to be bright if these talented playwrights are any indication."

While no group of eight plays can speak to all the concerns of a generation, this group does highlight several important aspects of life under thirty. Themes addressed include cultural/generational heritage, the value (or not) of work, and loss of innocence. The plays are also highly theatrical, taking place in such evocative settings as a '76 Maverick on an LA freeway, a rooftop in Minneapolis, and the middle of the South Pacific. In addition, the project brought an exciting generational continuity to the Humana Festival, since many of the *Life Under 30* playwrights have studied with former Humana playwrights, including Marsha Norman, Eduardo Machado and Elizabeth Wong.

The running order of *Life Under 30* was as follows:

*Slop-Culture* by Robb Badlam
*Mpls. St. Paul* by Julia Jordan
*Drive Angry* by Matt Pelfrey
*Just Be Frank* by Caroline Williams
—Intermission—
*Dancing with a Devil* by Brooke Berman
*Forty Minute Finish* by Jerome Hairston
*The Blue Room* by Courtney Baron
*Labor Day* by Sheri Wilner

The eight playwrights were joint recipients of the 1998 Heideman Award.

*—Ilana M. Brownstein*

# SLOP-CULTURE

by

## Robb Badlam

## SLOP-CULTURE
**by Robb Badlam**
Directed by Maria Mileaf

## CAST

*Brian:* Bryan Richards
*Dylan:* Derek Cecil
*Danielle:* Monica Koskey
*Cindy:* Carolyn Baeumler

Scenic Designer: Paul Owen
Costume Designer: Michael Oberle
Lighting Designer: Mimi Jordan Sherin
Sound Designer: Darron L. West
Properties Designer: Mark Walston
Stage Manager: Heather Fields
Assistant Stage Managers: Dyanne M. McNamara,
Alyssa Hoggatt
Dramaturgs: Amy Wegener, Sara Skolnick
Casting: Laura Richin Casting

## SETTING
The present. New York

## SLOP-CULTURE

*(DYLAN and BRIAN, a pair of 20-somethings wearing their finest bumming-around-the-house clothes, are on the couch, in the midst of a heated discussion.)*

BRIAN. Oh, come on!

DYLAN. Can't do it.

BRIAN. That's my answer!

DYLAN. Inadmissible.

BRIAN. But it's true!

DYLAN. Our judges have spoken: The Pillsbury Dough Boy cannot be your role model.

BRIAN. Why not? Poke me in the stomach! I'll giggle!

DYLAN. Judges say: "Talk to the hand, girlfriend."

BRIAN. *(Very put out.)* Man! *(Pause.)* What about Fred from *Scooby-Doo*?

DYLAN. That, we'll accept.

BRIAN. Fred and not Pop'n'Fresh?

DYLAN. It's really for your own good.

BRIAN. *(Resigned.)* Man!

*(A pause. A grin creeps across BRIAN's face.)*

BRIAN. *(Nodding.)* Dude ... Daphne.

DYLAN. *(Complete agreement.)* Aaaww yeah. You know Fred was givin' her the business in the back of the Mystery Machine.

BRIAN. Aaaaaww yeeeaah. *(Beat. Impressed.)* Fred, man. He was one smooth operator. Had his own sense of style.

DYLAN. Not many guys could pull off the white shirt and ascot and still look tough.

*(They nod a moment. A pause.)*

    BRIAN. You think Shaggy and Velma ever hooked up?
    DYLAN. *(With certainty.)* When they were drunk.

*(DANIELLE enters. She has a packet of papers in one hand. She is dressed professionally, but she is very jittery and nervous.)*

    DANIELLE. Hey guys. Cindy here?
    BRIAN. *(Calling over his shoulder.)* Cindy! Your lawyer's here!
    DANIELLE. *(Instantly paranoid.)* Shit! Do I really look like a lawyer? Shit! I need to look like a personnel coordinator! Shit! A lawyer? Shit! Really?
    BRIAN. You could be Marcia Clark's twin.
    DYLAN. Dude, that's cold.
    BRIAN. Oh, sorry. You'd be the younger, less weathered twin.
    DYLAN. *(To DANIELLE.)* So what's with the new look? Witness Relocation?
    DANIELLE. I'm applying for a job.
    DYLAN. Whoa! Whoa! Whoa! I object, Your Honor! *(Steps onto a chair.)* Hear now these words I say: Under no circumstances ... I say again for emphasis ... *no circumstances* ... are you to maintain or operate a frozen yogurt dispenser. Learn from my mistakes, Danielle ... I have permanent scars. Let this be a lesson ... look on my twisted form and learn ...

*(DYLAN starts to undo his pants.)*

    DANIELLE. No!
    DYLAN. My life is nothing if not cautionary example.
    DANIELLE. It's an office job!

*(Pause.)*

    DYLAN. No frozen yogurt?
    DANIELLE. No!

*(Pause.)*

    DYLAN. Soft serve?
    DANIELLE. Dylan! It's an office.

*(Pause.)*

DYLAN. *(Contemplative.)* I see. *(Pause.)* So ... no dessert or snack vending of any kind?

DANIELLE. *(Emphatic.)* It's an OFFICE!

BRIAN. *(Offering.)* I got my hand caught inside the VCR once. *(Beat.)* I got it out.

DANIELLE. *(Frustrated, to DYLAN.)* Is ... your sister ... home!?

DYLAN. Shower.

*(He points vaguely down the hallway. Much on her mind, DANIELLE exits in that direction.)*

DYLAN. Okay. One line. Summarize the show. *Dukes of Hazzard.* Go.

BRIAN. "Kew! Kew! Kew! Fuck you, Duke boys!"

DYLAN. Rosco never said "fuck."

BRIAN. That was his subtext. You go. *Gilligan's Island.*

DYLAN. "Gilligan! Drop those coconuts!" BONK! "Oow!"

*(Pause.)*

BRIAN. Whoa. *(Pause.)* Nice. *(Pause.)* I could see the coconuts.

DYLAN. It's a gift.

*(CINDY enters, bathrobe, towel, drying her hair. She is late and in a hurry. DANIELLE, like a small yap dog, is hot on her heels.)*

CINDY. Danni, I can't do this now. I'm late as it is. If I'm late one more time, the agency is going to fire me. Do you realize how difficult it is to get fired by a temp agency?

*(CINDY brushes her hair in front of a mirror. She continues dressing and preparing throughout.)*

DANIELLE. I need your help!

CINDY. *(Resigned.)* Talk.

DANIELLE. They want me to answer this essay question ...

CINDY. What's the question?

DANIELLE. ... And I don't think my answer is going to be what they're looking for ...

CINDY. What's the question?

DANIELLE. ... In fact, I'm sure it's not what they're looking for ...

CINDY. What's the damn question?!

DANIELLE. Cindy, did you ever go to church as a kid?

CINDY. That's the question?

DANIELLE. No. I'm asking. Did you ever go to church?

CINDY. Nope. My Sunday afternoons started with Abbot and Costello, and ended with Godzilla. God bless Channel 11. Why?

DANIELLE. Just curious.

CINDY. Thinking of finding Jesus?

DYLAN. And the conversation turns to matters of great import.

BRIAN. I met a Jewish guy once. *(They look at him. He continues, deflated.)* I don't really have a story to go with that.

*(The conversation swerves back to DANIELLE.)*

CINDY. Ignore that man behind the curtain. Why do you ask, Danni?

DANIELLE. Sometimes I ... *(Unsure, but pushes ahead.)* ... Well ... there's this Baptist Church ... in my neighborhood ... and ... sometimes go and ... I just ... I sit outside and listen.

CINDY. To what?

DANIELLE. The singing. It's nice.

CINDY. Why don't you go in?

DANIELLE. I couldn't. I don't ... I don't belong.

CINDY. *(Stops. Looks at her.)* Are you okay, Danni?

DANIELLE. They've got something. I can't put my finger on it, but ... *(Searching for words.)* ... It's ... I don't know. They've got—

DYLAN. Milk?

BRIAN. The music in them?

DYLAN. The fever for the flavor of a Pringle?

CINDY. *(Threatening them.)* Don't make me turn this car around.

BRIAN. *(Intimidated.)* We'll be good.

*(Pause.)*

DANIELLE. They've got a past.

*(Pause.)*

CINDY. How do you figure?

DANIELLE. A past. A history. They came from somewhere.

CINDY. Did we spontaneously self-generate this afternoon, Master Yoda?

DANIELLE. It's different. It's something we don't have. It's a sense of ... I don't know ... community?

CINDY. What was college?

DANIELLE. Yeah, but don't you see? College pulls you out of one community, changes you, and forces you into a new one. Then, as soon as you get comfortable, that new community gets jerked out from under your feet after four years.

BRIAN. Six years.

DANIELLE. And where does that leave you? You're a different person now. You can't go backwards. You can't go back home. Because home isn't where you left it. It's different. *You're* different. You don't really fit in anymore. You don't have anything to hang onto. It's like you're ... I don't know ... marooned.

DYLAN. *Gilligan's Island.*

CINDY. *(Scolding.)* Dylan.

DYLAN. *(On to something.)* No, I'm serious. That's the reason the Professor could build a satellite out of coconuts and twine, but he couldn't patch the hole in the boat. They're spiritual castaways. They can't go back to the mainland because they don't belong there anymore. The island has changed them fundamentally. They *are* home. They just won't accept it because they can't see it. Where they most want to go, they already are. It's very Zen. They hate the island, but it's part of them. They can't deny it. You can take the boy away from the coconuts but you can't take the coconuts away from the boy.

BRIAN. Coconuts. The great social equalizer.

*(Pause.)*

CINDY. Dylan?

DYLAN. Yes?

CINDY. Never speak again.

DANIELLE. *(Producing paper.)* What's your earliest and fondest childhood memory?

CINDY. What?

DANIELLE. That's the question. "What's your earliest and fondest childhood memory and what impact do you think the experience has had on you as a person?" *(Beat.)* I need yours. Mine sucks.

*(Pause.)*

CINDY. *(Thinking.)* Hmm. McDonald's cheeseburger. *(Beat.)* Fridays used to be the big night. Mom would take us to McDonald's as a treat. We'd get all dressed up. She'd put those Happy Meals in front of us and we thought we were at the Ritz Carlton having caviar.

DYLAN. Uh-huh. And you used to tell me that Shamrock Shakes were made out of Grimace's brain juice. I've never forgiven you for that.

CINDY. I'd have been derelict in my duties as Older Sister if I didn't terrorize you.

BRIAN. My folks got divorced when I was three. I don't remember it. I always used to wish Fonzie was my real dad. *(Beat.)* Then I'd cry because the Cunninghams made him live in the garage. So I'd leave cookies in our garage. Then the raccoons came ...

CINDY. So what's your memory, Danni?

DANIELLE. I can't ...

CINDY. Come on.

DANIELLE. It's totally wrong!

CINDY. What is it?

DANIELLE. Do you remember in the opening credits for *Tom & Jerry*? When Tom's sticking his tongue out? And the big bulldog pounds him on top of the head and makes him bite his tongue off?

CINDY. Yeah. *(DANIELLE is quiet.)* That's IT? That's your earliest, fondest memory?

DANIELLE. *(Smiles.)* Tom looks so embarrassed about it!

CINDY. I could be wrong, but I think that's probably on that big list of things NOT to write on your job application.

DANIELLE. I know! *(Beat.)* But it's true. *(Pause.)* Cindy, when my mom was my age she was cooking huge Sunday dinners with her entire family ... all the aunts and uncles and cousins and grandparents ... they all lived right there in the same neighborhood! Like their own little Sicilian embassy in the middle of Brooklyn! *(Beat.)* But then my mom moved away and got married and started her own family ... and I grew up in the suburbs. *(Beat.)* I was a kid eating Crunch Berries over *Schoolhouse Rock* at the same age when my mom and my great-great-great-grandmother were making ... *(Searching.)* ... baklava!

CINDY. Isn't baklava Greek?

DANIELLE. See! *(Beat.)* Cindy, I'm half Italian, and I need help ordering spaghetti at the Olive Garden!

BRIAN. If it helps, I've lost touch with my Viking heritage, too.

CINDY. *(To BRIAN.)* Don't make me come over there.

DANIELLE. So what do I do? I can't write down the truth. They'll think I'm four years old. I mean, I AM! I might as well be! I feel totally out of place going into an office! Like I've snuck in with my mom's blazer and my dad's briefcase. Petrified they're going to find me out! That they're gonna suddenly look up at me and say, "Silly rabbit! Job's are for grownups!"

CINDY. So you want my advice?

DANIELLE. YES!

CINDY. Lie.

*(CINDY moves swiftly off in the direction of the back bedroom.)*

DANIELLE. No shit! How? *(Following her halfway.)* I wanted to use yours, but cheeseburgers and ... and ... Fonzie's brain juice aren't on *Fortune 500*'s big list of "do's" either!

*(CINDY re-enters, dressed and ready. Bag in hand, she is out the door.)*

CINDY. I really wish I could be more help, sweetie, but if I don't leave right now, I'll be filling out job applications too. Relax. Be creative. Good luck.

*(A quick peck on the cheek and CINDY is gone. A pause. DANIELLE stares at the door. Then, lets out a frustrated scream.)*

DYLAN. Don't deny the island, Danni.

DANIELLE. What?!

DYLAN. Your past. Your history.

BRIAN. Your coconuts.

DYLAN. Where the castaways most want to go, they already are. The island. It's part of them. Like it or not.

BRIAN. Dude, didn't Gilligan get arrested for dope?

DYLAN. That's not helping the metaphor, man.

BRIAN. Sorry.

DYLAN. So what if our cultural heritage is only twenty-five years of bad TV. It's not much, but it's something. Embrace it. It's ours.

BRIAN. *(Serious.)* Gilligan, drop those coconuts.

DYLAN. *(Serious.)* Bonk.

BRIAN. *(Serious.)* Ow.

*(Pause.)*

DANIELLE. *(With a faint smile.)* Yeah.

DYLAN. Be proud, Danielle. You go right ahead and bite off that cartoon cat's tongue.

BRIAN. Hear! Hear!

DYLAN. *(To BRIAN.)* I think our work here is done. *(Motions to door.)* Shall we?

BRIAN. Indubitably! *(BRIAN and DYLAN get up and start out.)* Dude, we got nowhere to go.

DYLAN. *(Without breaking stride.)* Doesn't matter.

*(They're gone. DANIELLE, alone, sits thinking. Then takes up her pen and begins to write—with confidence. A smile creeps across her face. For the first time, she is relaxed. A weight's been lifted—more than the application.)*

DANIELLE. *(Laughing.)* No way I'm getting this job.

*(DANIELLE keeps writing. Blackout.)*

**END OF PLAY**

# MPLS., ST. PAUL

by

## Julia Jordan

*For Justin Kirk*

## MPLS., ST. PAUL
### by Julia Jordan
Directed by Abby Epstein

### CAST
*Mel:* Erica Blumfield
*Billy:* C. Andrew Bauer

Scenic Designer: Paul Owen
Costume Designer: Michael Oberle
Lighting Designer: Mimi Jordan Sherin
Sound Designer: Darron L. West
Properties Designer: Mark Walston
Stage Manager: Heather Fields
Assistant Stage Managers: Dyanne M. McNamara,
Alyssa Hoggatt
Dramaturgs: Michael Bigelow Dixon, Adrien-Alice Hansel
Casting: Laura Richin Casting

### CAST
Billy: seventeen years old
Mel: seventeen years old

### SET
On a slanted roof in the summertime.

## MPLS., ST. PAUL

*(BILLY and MEL are climbing out a window onto the roof.)*

BILLY. I did!

MEL. Bull-Crap.

BILLY. And Stinson was wailing away. I turned ...

MEL. Lie.

BILLY. He was wailing away on that guitar ...

MEL. *(With her hands over her ears.)* Na-na-na-na-na-na—Can't hear lies. Don't hear little boy lies.

BILLY. Just 'cause you weren't there ...

MEL. Neither were you.

BILLY. ... doesn't make it not true.

MEL. Yes it does.

BILLY. In your mind. I sang with The Replacements last night at 7th St. Entry. End of fuckin' story. And you're jealous.

MEL. I don't wanna sing with The Replacements.

BILLY. Sure you do.

MEL. No. I don't.

BILLY. You wanna get close to them. And I got closer than you'll ever get. I got inside the best song from the best rock album ever released, which just happens to be by the Replacements.

MEL. Who's Alex Chilton?

BILLY. An influence.

MEL. Yeah, but who?

BILLY. I don't know.

MEL. 1967, he was sixteen, his band The Boxtops had a number one with "The Letter." At nineteen he formed Big Star and they released "#1 Record" which never went near number one. Then "Radio City." They never played Radio City. And "3rd Record." But no one cared! So he recorded his fuck you album "Like Flies on Sherbet." The Replacements love "Flies on Sherbet." One critic said it sounded like a "bunch of drunken louts running amok...."

BILLY. Your brother told you that.

MEL. No. I just know! I was born knowing! He's not their biggest fan. I am.

BILLY. He's their fattest fan. Maybe he was there. The fat slob standing at the back so as he won't get hurt and all of a sudden whose on stage singin' his favorite song, "Favorite Thing"? Me. That's who. Me.

MEL. You better stop tellin' your tired old lie or I'm gonna push you off the roof.

BILLY. Girl, if you wanna touch me you don't have to come up with an excuse like that. You wanna touch the man that sang with The Placemats?

MEL. Shut up.

BILLY. I haven't bathed.

MEL. Ugh.

BILLY. Still got their sweat on my skin. Rock sweat. Mine and Paul Westerberg's. He was right next to me. This close. He handed me the microphone with his SWEAT on it. Hand to hand. You know what I'm sayin'? And then Bobby spun 'round and a whole truckload of it whipped cross my chest. Which do you want to touch first? Hand or chest? What do you want first? Mine and Paul's sweat? Or Bobby's and mine?

MEL. Only Paul's. Thanks.

BILLY. We should start our own band. You can be the singer.

MEL. Can't sing.

BILLY. We could write the songs together and I'll play guitar.

MEL. You don't know how to play the guitar.

BILLY. Anybody can play the guitar. It ain't easy but it ain't hard. The Replacements don't know how to play.

MEL. Yeah, but you suck.

BILLY. Bobby Stinson sucks.

MEL. I mean *really.*

BILLY. Tommy Stinson really sucks.

MEL. Yeah but The Replacements are geniuses at sucking. You suck ... generally.

BILLY. You could be Chrissie Hynde.

MEL. I don't want to be Chrissie Hynde.

BILLY. Who do you want to be then?

MEL. Paul's girlfriend.

BILLY. Well, you're not. You're mine.

MEL. I am not.

BILLY. We spend every day together. We sleep together when your 'rents are outta town.

MEL. Do we fuck?

BILLY. You're a virgin.

MEL. So are you. So I'm just a girl and your friend. Like that. I'm gonna be Paul's *girlfriend.*

BILLY. You wanna fuck Paul?

MEL. You taken that Mensa test yet?

BILLY. How do you know you want to, when you don't even know what it is, the thing you say you want to do?

MEL. I know.

BILLY. How?

MEL. I know because when he sings, "you're my favorite thing bar nothin'," I can feel him singin' it to me.

BILLY. He doesn't sing it. He yells it.

MEL. I get this shudder.

BILLY. He's already got a girlfriend. She's in a band.

MEL. Her time's up.

BILLY. If you and me were in a band we could open for them. Meet them.

MEL. I don't want to be in a band. Who wants girls in a band?

BILLY. What do you have against rock chicks?

MEL. I got nothin' against them. I just don't want to fuck them.

BILLY. Well, I do.

MEL. Well, that's not gonna happen even if I was in your band.

BILLY. I was talking about the Go-Gos.

MEL. That's not gonna happen either.

BILLY. But you're gonna do Paul Westerberg.

MEL. Right.

BILLY. How?

MEL. The old-fashioned way. Jump him.

BILLY. My friend Paul? We're friends now. Me and Paul. Yep. After The Entry we all went over to Liquor Lyles, me and Paul, Tommy, Bobby, and Chris Mars and all our hangers-on ... bunch of girls like you that we ignored. We all went over there and met up with Paul's super hot-*rocker*-girlfriend. Not girl and friend. Like that. But *girlfriend* as in the only girl he wants to fuck.

MEL. OK. First of all. How could you get into The Entry anyway? You're underage.

BILLY. Back door when the bouncer stepped away. Hid in the boiler room from four in the afternoon till ten-thirty. Which is when I heard the beatific tones of "Gary's Got A Boner" and slyly segued my underage ass into the crowd and pushed my way up, front and center.

MEL. Uh huh. And how did you get into Liquor Lyles? They card at the door.

BILLY. They don't card when you come in with God and they

don't card when you come in with The Replacements. Impressed now, huh? You wanna touch me now?

MEL. The Replacements don't hang out at Liquor Lyles. If you were a true fan you'd know that. They hang out at the CC Club. "The bar with casual elegance." Even my brother knows that.

BILLY. OK. Fine. We didn't go to Liquor Lyles. But I did get into The Entry, and I did jump up on stage and I did sing. I sang "Favorite Thing." And when I got to "BAR NOTHING" Paul stood back 'cause I was doin' him proud and Bobby ... Bobby Stinson just wailed away on that guitar. For one song. One rendition, in their hometown, of the best song off the best album of rock ever released, and ever to be released, and I was in the band. I was a Replacement.

MEL. So ... you don't know if he has a girlfriend or not.

BILLY. I know it's not you.

MEL. Well, it's gonna be.

BILLY. How come you do that huh?

MEL. Do what?

BILLY. Shoot me down.

MEL. I'm just sitting here. Wanna get high?

BILLY. NO! I'M TALKING HERE ABOUT OUR RELATION-SHIP WHICH HAPPENS TO BE VERY IMPORTANT TO ME. WELL, OK BUT LATER. It's important to you too, isn't it?

MEL. 'Course. My brother's gonna be home by six and it'll take a good half hour to find it. He rehid it. I think he's weighing it. We gotta get slier.

BILLY. It'll take twenty minutes tops to find it. So listen to me!

MEL. Alright you've got ten minutes.

BILLY. I don't know that I have ten minutes worth to say. It's just ...

MEL. What?

BILLY. I don't like it when you talk about them like that.

MEL. Who?

BILLY. The Replacements.

MEL. Like what? Like I love and adore them? Like sometimes when people, like my fat brother, really piss me off, I mean really, like there'll never be another fun time in my whole life, ever, like they save me a little? A LOT. Like they are a huge massive part of my life and always will be? Like that? Like when I talk about them like that? You don't like that? Like how the fuck do you think you sound?

BILLY. When you say you want to fuck Paul. I don't like that.

MEL. You said you wanted too the Go-Gos and don't go thinkin' I don't know exactly which one you mean.

BILLY. I'm not lettin' her stand between us.

MEL. Her who? Go-Go *Jane*?

BILLY. I said shut up.

MEL. Jane far far away in Califor-ni-ay?

BILLY. I'm being serious.

MEL. So am I. I'm real serious about Paul. *He lives here.* In reality. Someday I'll walk down the street and bang, smack into him. I could just bang into him.

BILLY. If you had any balls you'd just take the bus downtown to The Entry ... Why can't we sleep together?

MEL. We do.

BILLY. You know what I mean.

MEL. Fuck?

BILLY. Don't use that word with us.

MEL. Because.

BILLY. Because why?

MEL. Because I love you.

BILLY. What?

MEL. You're my best ... my ... well ... you just are. It's true. Can we get high now?

BILLY. You're not making any sense.

MEL. Oh fuck off. I said it didn't I?

BILLY. You never said it before. I thought that's why.... Because you didn't. Every time before when I said it. When I said to you. All you said back was "thank you."

MEL. I was grateful.

BILLY. But you did? All along?

MEL. I don't know about "all along." I don't know when it started. It just sort of occurred to me. After it was already there. Sorta.

BILLY. Why didn't you tell me?

MEL. I just did! Can we get high now? My brother's gonna be home soon.

BILLY. But we're not gonna ...

MEL. No.

BILLY. Why not?

MEL. 'Cause that would seal the deal and I've got things to do before I sign on any dotted line.

BILLY. I'm not askin' you to sign anything.

MEL. Yes you are.

BILLY. No I'm not.

MEL. I have things to do.

BILLY. Like Paul Westerberg.

MEL. And other things. All sorts of things.

BILLY. Without me.

MEL. I'm never gonna find anybody else. Not like you. I'm never gonna be able to say to anyone else, "Remember? Remember when we used to get high up on the roof and talk about, you lie about, The Replacements?" Nobody but you. You'll always be my favorite. This will always be my favorite time. We're never gonna forget this. 'Cause it's so stupid and great. Mythic even. To us at least. And that's enough. That'll be enough to pull us back together after we get our alone stuff done. That's what I think. So that's why. I'm gonna go find his pot. Thank God he still lives at home at the age of twenty-four. Beller when you see the fat bastard's car.

*(MEL climbs back in through the window.)*

BILLY. I'm her favorite thing. *"Bar nothin'."* Fuck Paul. I sang it better than he ever did. He knew it.

*(Lights change, giving BILLY a private rock star moment as he rocks out on the memory.)*

**END OF PLAY**

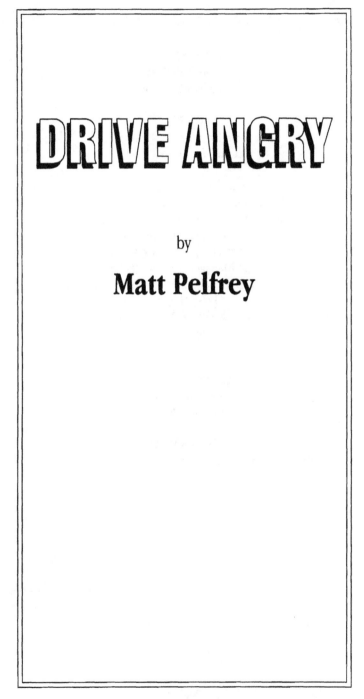

# DRIVE ANGRY

by

## Matt Pelfrey

## DRIVE ANGRY
### by Matt Pelfrey
Directed by Abby Epstein

### CAST
*Chemo-Boy:* Bryan Richards
*Rex the Mex:* Derek Cecil

Scenic Designer: Paul Owen
Costume Designer: Michael Oberle
Lighting Designer: Mimi Jordan Sherin
Sound Designer: Darron L. West
Properties Designer: Mark Walston
Stage Manager: Heather Fields
Assistant Stage Manager: Dyanne M. McNamara,
Alyssa Hoggatt
Dramaturgs: Michael Bigelow Dixon, Ilana M. Brownstein
Casting: Laura Richin Casting

### CHARACTERS
Chemo-Boy: Male, 20s
Rex the Mex: Male, 20s

### TIME and PLACE
Night in Los Angeles. A thundering '76 Maverick.

# DRIVE ANGRY

*(REX THE MEX behind the wheel. CHEMO-BOY rides shotgun.)*

REX THE MEX. Concrete, concrete, concrete ...

CHEMO-BOY. My dad stopped by yesterday ...

REX THE MEX. ... lights, neon, billboards ...

CHEMO-BOY. ... out of nowhere. Just, like, I'm chillin', then KNOCK KNOCK KNOCK, I'm like, "Oh, shit, who's that ..."

REX THE MEX. ... rich cars, poor cars, ugly cars, dented cars, cars with tint, cars with out-of-state plates, cars with vanity plates...

CHEMO-BOY. ... so I open the front door and there's my old-ster, and he gets in my face, he's like, "How you doin' kiddo?"

REX THE MEX. ... cars with loser zoos, cars with stupid bumper stickers, cars with no bumpers, hot rods, jeeps, vans, busses ...

CHEMO-BOY. And I swear to Christ, I almost pass out—his breath smelled like *seaweed...*

REX THE MEX. Asian dudes, Armenian dudes, Arab dudes, black dudes, brown dudes, white dudes ... everyone mixing, merging, honking ...

CHEMO-BOY. ... like there was this sick, repugnant *stew* brewing in his mouth...

REX THE MEX. Like this freeway is just a big concrete blood-stream full of mechanical germs ... angry mechanical germs ...

CHEMO-BOY. So he comes in and we talk, same old shit, then he asks me if I've got any soup ... and I tell him I got plenty of soup. So now he's there for like, five minutes only and he already wants me to cook for him. So I tell him I got Minestrone and I got Fiesta Bean, but that's not good enough, he wants Vegetable Beef. So I'm like, "Man, just have Minestrone," and so that's what I cook up. So I give him a bowl with some crackers, and he just clams up. Stops talkin'. He just sits there, staring at his soup, brooding. Y'know? Just like, in a funk. This hideous soup-funk. So I said,

183

basically, unless you got money to help me with my medical bills, you can fuckin' get lost. So that's what he did. He split. Didn't touch his soup. Swear to Christ, I wanted to beat him over the head with his prosthetic arm.

REX THE MEX. Your old man sounds like a disaster.

CHEMO-BOY. He's lived in a motel for two years.

REX THE MEX. So? He's a desperate, volatile maverick! He's on the edge!

CHEMO-BOY. But it's by choice...

REX THE MEX. What is?

CHEMO-BOY. His motel life-style. He has settlement money from the accident. I know he does.

REX THE MEX. So wait—he's holding out on you? He's got loot?

CHEMO-BOY. I think so.

REX THE MEX. See, *that* I got a problem with.

*(They drive in silence for a moment.)*

CHEMO-BOY. I hear some scientist in Seattle found Sasquatch hairs..

REX THE MEX. Fuck's a Sasquatch hair?

CHEMO-BOY. Sasquatch is another name for Bigfoot.

REX THE MEX. And some scientist has its hair?

CHEMO-BOY. Well actually, they think they're pubes...

REX THE MEX. Hold on. Sasquatch is covered, head-to-toe, in hair. Correct?

CHEMO-BOY. Yes.

REX THE MEX. Then follow me here: how do you know which hairs are his normal hairs, and which are his pubes?

CHEMO-BOY. When experts say they got Bigfoot's pubes, you take a statement like that at face value. *(Beat.)* Check it: initial tests show it's definitely some sort of non-human primate.

REX THE MEX. *(Repeating to himself.)* ... primate...

CHEMO-BOY. A primate's an ape.

REX THE MEX. I know what a primate is...

CHEMO-BOY. That's so cool. I hope it exists.

REX THE MEX. Bigfoot?

CHEMO-BOY. Yeah.

REX THE MEX. Why would you give a shit if Bigfoot exists or not?

CHEMO-BOY. I'd hunt it.

REX THE MEX. Get outta here ...

CHEMO-BOY. No, man, I would. Chase its ass, blow it away,

skin the bastard, make a cool rug. Sell the meat to Burger King or
Arby's. *(Pause.)* Can you give me a lift tomorrow?

REX THE MEX. Where to?

CHEMO-BOY. Where do you think?

REX THE MEX. What time?

CHEMO-BOY. Gotta be there by nine.

REX THE MEX. *(Slightly annoyed.)* Yeah, I can give you a ride.

CHEMO-BOY. Hey I don't wanna put you *out* or anything ...

REX. THE MEX. Just wanted to sleep in.

CHEMO-BOY. So fuck off. I'll find a ride.

REX THE MEX. I'll drive you.

CHEMO-BOY. No, really...

REX THE MEX. ... said I'd drive you...

CHEMO-BOY. Hey, you got *sleeping* to do.

REX THE MEX. I said I would fuckin' drive you, okay? Stop
sniveling.

CHEMO-BOY. I'm not sniveling.

REX THE MEX. You are. You're sniveling like some kinda
*victim.*

CHEMO-BOY. Shut up...

REX THE MEX. Little Chemo-Boy suffering from
cancer.Waaa!

CHEMO-BOY. Fuck off.

REX THE MEX. You're not even losing your *hair.*

CHEMO-BOY. What's that supposed to mean?

REX THE MEX. You know what it means.

CHEMO-BOY. No. I don't. Fuckin' tell me.

REX THE MEX. I mean, you know, what kind of wimpy cancer you got that your chemo doesn't make you go bald? You know?
On TV, all the cool cancer patients go bald.

CHEMO-BOY. My stuff doesn't do that.

REX THE MEX. ... 'Cause you got pussy chemo.

CHEMO-BOY. I implore you to fuck off. You're being a dick.

REX THE MEX. I'm chemo for your manhood.

CHEMO-BOY. You're *what*?

REX THE MEX. You heard me. I'm like, chemo for your, whatever, yeah, your manhood. I won't let you become one of those people
who start to feed off their disease. My uncle got pancreatic cancer,
and that's what he became. Pancreatic Cancer Man. Everything was
about his disease. How he's "bravely battling cancer." All that disease hype. The whole time, I'm thinking, what's so fucking brave
about battling something that you have no choice about? You got
cancer. You deal with it. It's like how we treat cops and firemen.
They save someone, they catch a killer, and, yeah, that's great, but

it's their *job*. It's not like some civilian that risks his life to intervene and save someone. A cop or fireman has no choice. Doing that shit is no more than what's expected. It's their job. They're not being heroes, they're earning a paycheck and enjoying a privileged position in society.

CHEMO-BOY. Whatever.

*(Pause.)*

REX THE MEX. What you goin' in for?
CHEMO-BOY. Like you care.
REX THE MEX. Stop brooding ...

*(Pause.)*

CHEMO-BOY. You ever get a CAT-scan?
REX THE MEX. Fuck no.
CHEMO-BOY. Dude, they give you a bottle of this shit, it's like, this white, creamy stuff, you gotta drink it before going in, so your insides will show up when they take the picture ...
REX THE MEX. ... yeah ...
CHEMO-BOY. ... stuff, I'm not kidding, is like drinking *moose semen.*
REX THE MEX. ... not that you know what drinking moose semen is like ...
CHEMO-BOY. I'm using poetic imagery so a puny mind like yours can grasp the horror and complexity of what I'm saying.
REX THE MEX. I think I appreciate that.
CHEMO-BOY. You fuckin' better.
REX THE MEX. So ...
CHEMO-BOY. ... so that's what they're doing tomorrow. I'm drinking a pint of moose cum, then they're shooting iodine into my veins to find out if I got any creepy shit hiding out.
REX THE MEX. That's fucked up.
CHEMO-BOY. Yeah it is ...

*(Pause. REX THE MEX thinks about something.)*

REX THE MEX. Let me ask you a question. Let me pose a thought to you ...
CHEMO-BOY. Please do.
REX THE MEX. Why did you get cancer?

*(Slight pause.)*

CHEMO-BOY. I don't know.

REX THE MEX. But what did the doctors tell you?

CHEMO-BOY. It could be any one of five hundred reasons.

REX THE MEX. But at your age, ass-cancer is rare.

CHEMO-BOY. Extremely.

REX THE MEX. So why did this shit grow inside of you?

CHEMO-BOY. I just told you—I don't fuckin' know.

REX THE MEX. Yeah? Well I *do.*

CHEMO-BOY. Oh, great.

REX THE MEX. I do, man. I really do.

CHEMO-BOY. There is no way on God's green earth you know anything my doctors don't know.

REX THE MEX. What you continually fail to grasp, my diseased little friend, is that I am not burdened by over-education. I haven't spent eight years after high school getting taught how to think and what pre-packaged crock of shit to spout so that I appear smart at parties and espresso bars. I actually think. I have forced myself to remain open to the Cosmic Whatever.

CHEMO-BOY. "The Cosmic Whatever?"

REX THE MEX. That's right ...

CHEMO-BOY. Alright—what's your diagnosis?

REX THE MEX. Existential pollution.

CHEMO-BOY. What the fuck is that?

REX THE MEX. All the shit out there. All the shit that pisses you off and eats at you day in and day out. All that shit has crawled up inside your ass and died like a sick rat. And that got everything infected.

CHEMO-BOY. And the shit is ... ?

REX THE MEX. Well, as I touched on already—the chicks that piss us off, our bullshit jobs, our fucking parents and especially the psychotic, selfish, assholic drivers who plague us every day of our lives. You see, all these elements are out there, like secondhand smoke—like *smog*—it's drifting, hanging in the air, contaminating our world. That's why our enforcement, our roadway counter-offensive against the scumbag fuckers of the world—that's why it's so important.

CHEMO-BOY. Hmmm ...

REX THE MEX. Am I right? You know I am.

CHEMO-BOY. It's food for thought.

REX THE MEX. It's a fucking all-you-can-eat buffet and it's all true.

CHEMO-BOY. Yeah it is.

REX THE MEX. *(Something grabs his attention.)* Here we go...

CHEMO-BOY. Where?

REX THE MEX. Next lane over.

CHEMO-BOY. Red truck?

REX THE MEX. Uh-huh.

CHEMO-BOY. What's the crime?

REX THE MEX. Merges like an a-hole, then cut across three lanes of traffic without signalling.

CHEMO-BOY. That is totally unacceptable behavior.

REX THE MEX. Agreed. *(REX accelerates. CHEMO-BOY produces a pellet handgun from under the seat.)* How's the pellet supply?

CHEMO-BOY. Doin' okay.

REX THE MEX. We need more?

CHEMO-BOY. We're cool.

REX THE MEX. Just tell me when.

CHEMO-BOY. I know the game.

REX THE MEX. Anyone behind us?

CHEMO-BOY. No.

REX THE MEX. Don't do it until just before the next off-ramp.

CHEMO-BOY. Who do you think you're talking to?

REX THE MEX. We can't get careless.

CHEMO-BOY. Don't worry about it.

REX THE MEX. Here it comes ...

CHEMO-BOY. It's time to administer some real medicine. Chemo for a tumorous city ...

REX THE MEX. Concentrate on the job at hand.

CHEMO-BOY. Shut up. I am. Here we go.

*(CHEMO-BOY leans out of the window, aims the pellet gun, fires three shots.*
*REX turns the steering wheel sharply towards the off-ramp.*
*Glass shatters.*
*Tires squeal.*
*Blackout.)*

**END OF PLAY**

# JUST BE FRANK

by

## Caroline Williams

## JUST BE FRANK
### by Caroline Williams
Directed by Maria Mileaf

## CAST
*Diane:* Carolyn Baeumler
*Charlene:* Monica Koskey
*Jan:* Caitlin Miller
*Secretary:* Erica Blumfield
*Boss:* Todd Cerveris

Scenic Designer: Paul Owen
Costume Designer: Michael Oberle
Lighting Designer: Mimi Jordan Sherin
Sound Designer: Darron L. West
Properties Designer: Mark Walston
Stage Manager: Heather Fields
Assistant Stage Managers: Dyanne M. McNamara,
Alyssa Hoggatt
Dramaturgs: Amy Wegener, Adrien-Alice Hansel
Casting: Laura Richin Casting

## CHARACTERS
DIANE
CHARLENE
JAN
SECRETARY
BOSS

## TIME & PLACE
The present. A busy office.

## JUST BE FRANK

*(Lights Up—Morning in a busy office.*
*Spotlights focus on two co-workers sitting at adjacent desks. Be-*
*hind them, other employees are periodically seen passing*
*through, miming office business or huddled around the water*
*cooler. At stage-left is a large reception desk and free-standing*
*closed door. Later, just beyond the door will be 'the boss's of-*
*fice'.*
*In the spotlight: CHARLENE, an attractive, overbearing young*
*professional, is wearing a garish, hot-pink suit and talking ani-*
*matedly with her dull-looking colleague, DIANE. In dress and*
*posture, DIANE is the mouse-like antithesis to CHARLENE's*
*in-your-face confidence. It's clear who dominates both their*
*work relationship and the conversation in progress.)*

CHARLENE. *(Striking a pose/modeling her new ensemble.)* It
looks expensive, doesn't it? I won't say how much ... but let me just
tell you ... if you even knew—you would *die. (Beat.) Five-hundred
dollars.* The saleslady said it looked incredible on me. You don't
think it's too loud, do you? She said I'd definitely stop traffic ...

DIANE. You *are* hard to miss. I mean, it is — *pink.*

CHARLENE. It's not *pink*, Diane, it's *salmon.* I want to look
professional when I approach the boss. I really think this suit says,
"I'm a woman. I'm not afraid to wear a salmon suit. I can be a
valuable asset to this company." *(Beat.)* That promotion has my
name written all over it .

*(CHARLENE wears a determined smile.)*

DIANE. You mean the Gaines Beefy-Treat account? I'm up for
that promotion ... I mean, I was thinking of applying. I thought

191

since my proposal saved the Ferber Cheese-Stick account last year ...

CHARLENE. Oh, that was *you. Well.* You should know that Ferber Cheese was child's play compared to Beefy Treats. *(Smiling 'helpfully'.)* You wouldn't want to be in over your head.

DIANE. *(Dejected.)* I guess you *are* more assertive than I am ... and confident. *(A beat, she looks at CHARLENE.)* And you stand out ...

CHARLENE. *(Condescendingly.)* Listen. Since you and I are friends—I'll be frank. *This* is the cutthroat world of business. *You* simply don't have any killer instinct and rarely do you ever have anything exciting to say. Not that those are *bad* qualities—you just lack *verve.*

DIANE. *Verve?*

CHARLENE. Don't worry—you still fulfill a very important role here. Where would people like *me* be without people like *you?* You're punctual and efficient and—meek.

DIANE. *(On the verge of tears.) Mm-meek?*

CHARLENE. *(Big, fake smile.)* In fact, you're *lucky we're such good friends* that we can be honest with each other because, for the most part, Diane, there is no place for honesty in business and not everyone will be as helpful as I am. Come to think of it, when I become president of this company, my first decree will be to have all of my people be *completely* honest—*all* of the time. *(She thinks.)* It will *revolutionize* the world of business. *(Beat.)* Sometimes my brilliance takes even me by surprise. *(CHARLENE is transfixed by her vision. Speechless, DIANE stares at her in disbelief. Emerging from her reverie, admiring herself, CHARLENE continues:)* Anyway, my suit *is* sensational, isn't it?

*(CHARLENE turns toward the water cooler, and is out of earshot by the time DIANE, her face contorting, manages to stammer under her breath.)*

DIANE. What do I know—I'm MEEK!

CHARLENE. *(Smiling over her shoulder, oblivious to DIANE's mounting rage.)* No need to thank me—

DIANE. *(Calling after her, sarcastic/bitter.)* Oh yeah, *THANKS*!!

*(DIANE turns angrily back to her computer and furiously begins to type.)*

*(Meanwhile, spotlights follow an obnoxiously cheerful CHARLENE to the water cooler where fellow employee, JAN, is standing alone, looking paranoid. Dressed in typical middle-manage-*

*ment attire [unflattering earth-tone blazer/skirt combo, "nude"
pantyhose and incongruous stark white tennis shoes], JAN holds
a paper Dixie-cup and speaks in a flat, nasal monotone. Her
face is an expressionless mask of resigned irritation and nau-
sea.)*

CHARLENE. Good morning, Jan. How was your weekend?

JAN. Absolute crap.

CHARLENE. Excuse me—?

JAN. I got stood up, my minivan blew a tire and I have a yeast
infection. Do you mind? I'm trying to look inconspicuous here
and you're standing next to me like a flashing pink beacon.

CHARLENE. *(Confused.)* Actually this suit is not pink, *Jan*,
it's *salmon*. What's gotten into you anyway? I'm counting on you
to nominate me for the new account. You're the only one the old
windbag ever listens to ...

JAN. Actually, *Charlene*, I'd feel better about *myself* if you'd
continue to earn substantially LESS than I do.

CHARLENE. *(Still confused.)* Are you trying to say you're *not*
going to give me the recommendation?

JAN. Listen, I'll be blunt. I don't like you. I've never liked you.
The way you are *constantly* waving at me from your desk—I have
to pretend like I'm writing or looking for something just to avoid
acknowledging you—but *you don't get it* ... you wave, I ignore
you and you keep flappin' away like ... some kind of—large, flight-
less bird.

CHARLENE. Well! *Excuuse me*, JAN!

JAN. *(Continuing—she could care less about CHARLENE's
objections.)* ... and, God help me if I ever sit next to you at a lunch
meeting again ... watching you eat could drive a person insane—
it's like watching one of those pointy-faced rodents—incessantly
pecking and pecking and ...

CHARLENE. *(Seething.)* Of all the rude ...

JAN. *(Continuing.)* ... and *speaking* of chewing—your last presentation was so mind-numbingly boring I actually had to *work* to
keep from gnawing off my own arm.

CHARLENE. I have heard just about ENOUGH thank-you-
very-much!

*(CHARLENE turns to leave.)*

JAN. Oh, in that case—before you go, the next time I sleep
with the boss in order to advance my own career, I'll be sure and
let slip that you called him a windbag ... Good luck!

*(JAN goes abruptly back to her desk.)*

CHARLENE. *(Calling lamely, after her.)* If that's the way you feel, then FINE—I'll meet with him *myself!*

*(CHARLENE stomps off to a large reception desk in front of a free-standing closed door inscribed with the word President in gold lettering. She addresses a perky, somewhat effeminate male SECRETARY who wears a constant, obsequious smile. Everything he says is delivered with a cheerful voice and genuinely eager, helpful attitude.)*

SECRETARY. *(Smiling warmly throughout.)* Hello, Ms. Parker. How can I kiss your ass today?
CHARLENE. ... excuse me?
SECRETARY. Would you like some coffee? This is regular but if you'd like decaf I'll just leave and come back with the same pot—you'll never know the difference.
CHARLENE. *(Confused.)* Uh—no. I just want to make an appointment with Mr. Ross ASAP.
SECRETARY. *(Checks appointment book, then looks up, still smiling.)* I'm sorry but I don't think he can squeeze you big pink ass in today. *(Cheerfully.)* Is there anything else I can help you with? *(CHARLENE's face reddens with anger. She is about to speak when the phone rings. SECRETARY turns to CHARLENE.)* Just a moment ... *(He holds up a finger to CHARLENE who waits, fuming. SECRETARY answers the phone.)* Burton and Ross, may I help you? ... today? ... with Mr. Ross? ... how about 2:15? ... all right then, buh-bye. *(Back to CHARLENE.)* As I was saying, are you sure there isn't anything else? I could go fetch some Post-its? Your dry-cleaning, perhaps? *(CHARLENE looks at him blankly, speechless.)* After all, what am I here to do if not *your* mindless, tedious busywork. Whatever you and all your *over-educated* colleagues with reserved parking and big pink suits think you're just too good for.

*(SECRETARY has a big smile.)*

CHARLENE. *(Enraged.)* FOR-YOUR-INFORMATION the suit is SALMON and I don't know what your *problem* is but I thought you said Mr. Ross was busy all day—*(Points to phone accusingly.)* What was that?!
SECRETARY. *(Explaining calmly, as if to a small child.)* No, I didn't say he was *busy*—I said I couldn't squeeze you in. He's

actually free until *(Glances down.)* 2:15. But, due to my inferiority complex and because this appointment book makes me drunk with power, I've decided to act out my passive-aggressive rage against you.

CHARLENE. *Excuse me* but I will *not* tolerate a secretary with that kind of attitu—

SECRETARY. *(Interrupting.)* That's *administrative maintenance engineer* and I would care what you were saying if you had any power at all in this company. Since you don't, I'll just smile and nod while I look for somebody important to suck up to ... Oh! There's an executive! If that will be all Ms. Parker ...

*(SECRETARY grabs the coffee pot and rushes off.)*

CHARLENE. *(Disgusted, to no one in particular.)* What is wrong with you people?!

*(CHARLENE walks past the desk to the boss's door and knocks, opening it gingerly, flooding his "office" with light. Inside sits MR. ROSS, flanked by stacks of files, behind an imposing oak desk. He wears a dark three-piece suit, red "power tie" and is slightly overweight with short hair and kind features. His tone and demeanor suggest an un-bearded, corporate Santa Claus.)*

CHARLENE. Mr. Ross?

MR. ROSS. *(Looking up from his paperwork.)* Yes? Come in.

CHARLENE. Hi, I was wondering if I could talk to you for a few minutes about a possible promotion on the new dog-treats account? Last month you had mentioned how I was really up-to-speed and I was thinking, what with my ...

MR. ROSS. *(Cutting her off, leaning back in his swivel-chair.)* Hmmm—yes, the Beefy Treats. You know, this is quite fascinating. I don't doubt that you do, in fact, work here and I may, indeed, have commented on your work ... I just can't for the life of me seem to remember who in the hell you are. What department did you say you work in?

CHARLENE. Um ... marketing and development.

MR. ROSS. Right, right—marketing. You must perform one of those benign tasks that, apparently, I see fit to dole out some measley, pissant salary for ... *(Cheerfully.)* in which case I suppose I should hear you out. You were saying ...?

CHARLENE. Uh ... well, I had actually come in here about a promotion but maybe now's not exactly the right time ...

MR. ROSS. *(Interrupting her with a sudden realization.)* Wait a minute! I do remember you—your desk is just across the way there...

*(MR. ROSS gestures past the door.)*

CHARLENE. *(Excited.)* Yes! That's me! Did you recall how I typed up those reports last term?

MR. ROSS. *(Cheerful and professional.)* Heavens no! I do recall, however, that I quite enjoy looking down your blouse on my way in here each morning ... and, considering that my taxes alone are probably twice what you make in an entire year—I suppose it wouldn't hurt to hand over an account I'll probably take credit for anyway. Congratulations Miss ...

CHARLENE. Parker ... Charlene Parker.

MR. ROSS. Of course. Congratulations Miss Proctor, the promotion is yours. *(Earnestly.)* Good luck and nice ass.

*(MR. ROSS gives CHARLENE a friendly thumbs-up [think enthusiastic Little League coach, "Nice catch!"] and promptly refocuses on his paperwork, effectively sending her on her way. CHARLENE is speechless. She walks slowly back to her desk, more than slightly disturbed.)*

DIANE. *(Bitterly.)* So, how'd it go?

CHARLENE. *(Suddenly crazed.)* GREAT, DI-ANE! As a matter of fact-WONDERFUL. *(Grotesquely enunciating each word.)* Did I not explain to you that a salmon suit like this would command RESPECT?

*(DIANE, startled, looks at CHARLENE like she is insane. After a moment, they turn to their respective computers and get to work.)*

**END OF PLAY**

# DANCING WITH A DEVIL

# A DEVIL

by

## Brooke Berman

## DANCING WITH A DEVIL
### by Brooke Berman
Directed by Abby Epstein

### THE CAST
*Woman:* Carolyn Baeumler
*Younger Woman:* Monica Koskey
*Man:* C. Andrew Bauer

Scenic Designer: Paul Owen
Costume Designer: Michael Oberle
Lighting Designer: Mimi Jordan Sherin
Sound Designer: Darron L. West
Properties Designer: Mark Walston
Stage Manager: Heather Fields
Assistant Stage Managers: Dyanne M. McNamara,
Alyssa Hoggatt
Dramaturgs: Amy Wegener, Sara Skolnick
Casting: Laura Richin Casting

### CHARACTERS
WOMAN
YOUNGER WOMAN
MAN

### PLACE
Here

### TIME
Now

## DANCING WITH A DEVIL

*(A WOMAN is on the stage. A YOUNGER WOMAN, the younger version of herself, is with her. The first woman talks to the audience. A MAN in a black turtleneck and black pants listens.)*

WOMAN. This is how it happens. I will tell it in the present tense so that you can be there with me. I will tell it in the present tense as if there were a way to reverse the story, to change the ending, so we can all hope together that it will be different.

YOUNGER WOMAN. I hate it when you tell it. It makes me feel afraid.

WOMAN. I am twenty-four years old and I live in New York City.

YOUNGER WOMAN. I really hate when you tell it. But I like the part before it happens. I like being young in New York.

I am twenty-four years old, and I live in New York City. My life is shiny and new and just barely discovered. I am an emerging something-or-other, waiting tables and writing stories. I go to parties with people whose skin sparkles and whose names are known. I like to tell stories about how I am twenty-four and still a virgin, deconstructing the relationship between my heart and my skin and my sex.

WOMAN. I was a virgin.

YOUNGER WOMAN. I like to dance, to feel air inside my body. I think that dancing will save me from pain. The music will Earth me and the beat will bring me to the ground. I go dancing in gay bars with funny names. I take great pleasure being a girl in a boy-bar, enjoying the fact that no one will try to pick me up. My life is safe. I play outrageous, but my life is safe. I have made it that way. Just enough outrage and lots of safety nets.

I live in an old apartment building in Soho, where the artists are, across the hall from a Mafia widow and next door to an idiot with a loud dog. I listen to the dog howl whenever he is alone. The sound of this drives me crazy and I complain about it but the owner does not listen.

On the first day of the new year, I write down a list of my dreams and goals. I have many dreams—the foremost of which is this: "I want to be transformed." I write it down, "I want to be transformed," because that is what I want.

I look for my transformation anywhere I can. I look for it in the eyes of other people, but do not see it there. I look for it in the mountains of New Mexico, in the water of the hot springs, in the air of New York City and in the words that come to me while I dream. I dream that I am leaving an old city and moving to a new one and going to film school and leaving my mother.

It is June, and I am twenty-four, and I am about to be transformed.

WOMAN. It is June, June 9th to be precise, just barely after midnight, and I am about to fall asleep in my safe bed, in my safe Soho fourth-floor walk-up.

It is four in the morning and I open my eyes, certain that Sarah, my old roommate, has come home, though she moved out months ago and this makes no sense, I am sure that Sarah is in the apartment and I open my eyes, fully believing that I will see her there.

But I don't see Sarah. I see someone I do not know. I open my eyes to a stranger standing at the foot of my bed wearing a little black half-mask and a black turtleneck, looking a little bit like Zorro or like an existentialist Lone Ranger and I cannot understand how this stranger has penetrated my sleep or entered my apartment.

YOUNGER WOMAN. I don't like this part.

WOMAN. The stranger just stares at me. He doesn't move. He says, "Good Evening."

MAN. Good evening.

WOMAN. And I say, Don't hurt me.

YOUNGER WOMAN. Don't hurt me.

WOMAN. And the stranger moves toward me, very very slowly like in slow motion and I understand everything that is about to happen. I understand it in my mind before he even touches me. I think, this can't happen to me. I think, this can't happen to me because I am very smart. I have read Roland Barthes and I know how to deconstruct sexuality. I am a virgin and I am very smart and things like this are not supposed to happen to people like me.

YOUNGER WOMAN. I really don't like this part.

MAN. I won't hurt you.

*(The YOUNGER WOMAN and the MAN start to dance—a very slow ballroom dance. They dance throughout the next beat.)*

WOMAN. He shows me the knife by running it across my ass so that I will feel that it is sharp and yet it leaves no mark. He leaves no mark. I will be taken to the hospital within an hour but there will be no mark that anything has happened to me.

YOUNGER WOMAN. But it is the present and I am not at the hospital yet. I am dancing with the devil right now in time that lasts longer than ordinary time. I say, "Please don't hurt me," and no one talks after that.

MAN. I won't hurt you.

YOUNGER WOMAN. I'm a virgin. I'm like the Virgin Mary. This can't happen to the Virgin Mary. And I think, You knew all along that this would happen to you. Who else were you saving yourself for?

MAN. You were saving yourself for me.

WOMAN. Maybe I was. How could I have known?

MAN. Everything will change now. Everything about you will change. You will no longer be who you were. You will have to become someone else to even understand this, to even put it behind you. You will leave your friends, your home, your family, in order to become the person who can put this behind herself. I am the answer to your prayers. I am giving you what you asked for. I am giving you the gift of transformation.

YOUNGER WOMAN. But I don't want to transform. Not like this. I don't want to go through with it.

MAN. You have no choice. You can fight me, or you can live.

WOMAN. I am light and light I shall remain. That is what I was told to say.

YOUNGER WOMAN. I am light and light I shall remain. I am in a time and place in which this event is not occurring. I am not in my body, and so you cannot touch me. You are filling me with your pain, with your body, but you are not touching me. You are not even near me, you are nowhere near me. I am held in the arms of angels and I am light, and light I shall remain.

*(The MAN and the YOUNGER WOMAN stop dancing. The MAN bows to the WOMAN and leaves the stage.)*

WOMAN. It was over quickly. It seemed to take a long time but I know that in the reality we will call reality, it happened within the span of ten, maybe fifteen minutes. He turned me over like some object and covered my head with a pillow and stuck his pain and his rage and his dick all inside me, and then it was over, and he was gone, as quietly and mysteriously as he came. He came out of the night and went back inside of it and was never caught.

YOUNGER WOMAN. He disappears. He is never caught. I run through the halls of my apartment building half-naked looking for help.

WOMAN. I do not want to see women get raped anymore. Not in the movies, not in the theater, not on TV and not in my bedroom. I do not want this experience. I do not want to see it and I do not want to relive it.

YOUNGER WOMAN. I am light and light I shall remain.

WOMAN. That's what the spirit guides told me to say. I am light and light I shall remain. I cannot be hurt. But I was hurt.

I have taken the pain of some man that I do not know inside of me. I have taken it inside and transformed it, inside. I have gone to rape crisis centers and to therapy and to psychic healings in order to transform the pain that you stuck inside me one morning, me a stranger. I carry energy inside of me, some of which you deposited there, and rapists do not use condoms.

But I am not a repository for some stranger's suffering. Do you hear me? I DON'T WANT YOUR SUFFERING. YOU CAN JUST PUT IT SOMEWHERE ELSE. AND I HOPE THAT YOU SUFFER TIL THE END OF TIME, TIL THE END OF EVERYTHING, MAY YOUR SOUL KNOW WHAT YOU HAVE DONE TO ME AND MAY YOU BE ... May you be healed.

YOUNGER WOMAN. I want to go home now.

WOMAN. We're almost done. We're almost at the end.

YOUNGER WOMAN. I'm hurt, and I want to go home.

WOMAN. I am going to tell it again.

YOUNGER WOMAN. Everything will change, he said. And it did. I did. Please don't tell it. I don't want to remember.

WOMAN. Everything will change, he said. Although he didn't really speak at all.

*(The MAN reappears.)*

MAN. Good evening ...

YOUNGER WOMAN. I want to go home now.

WOMAN. I am not twenty-four years old anymore. I do not know the people I knew then. My friends are different. My work is different. I have lived in seven different apartments in the span of three years. Everything has changed. I have changed.

YOUNGER WOMAN. Except that I still wake up at four in the morning expecting to find him there.

*(The MAN moves towards her.)*

MAN. You are one of the statistics. You are about to become a statistic. One of the numbers. How many women in ten?

YOUNGER WOMAN. I don't want to dance with you.

WOMAN. I'm not going to tell it again.

YOUNGER WOMAN. I just want to go home.

WOMAN. I am twenty-eight years old, and I still live in New York. I sleep with a nightlight. I do not live alone. I stay at other people's houses when my roommates are away. I do not watch movies in which women are tracked, killed, hurt, maimed, terrorized or raped. This means I do not watch a lot of movies. I meet young women who remind me of myself before it happened, and they scare me. I am afraid that something might happen to them too that will cause them to leave a piece of themselves behind forever. I hope this is not the case. I wish them well.

**END OF PLAY**

# FORTY MINUTE FINISH

by

**Jerome Hairston**

## FORTY MINUTE FINISH
### by Jerome Hairston
Directed by Maria Mileaf

### CAST
Ike: Derek Cecil
Terry: Nick Garrison

Scenic Designer: Paul Owen
Costume Designer: Michael Oberle
Lighting Designer: Mimi Jordan Sherin
Sound Designer: Darron L. West
Properties Designer: Mark Walston
Stage Manager: Heather Fields
Assistant Stage Manager: Dyanne M. McNamara,
Alyssa Hoggatt
Dramaturgs: Michael Bigelow Dixon, Ilana Brownstein
Casting: Laura Richin Casting

### CHARACTERS
Ike—a young grocery store clerk
Terry—a young grocery store clerk

### TIME
The present

### SETTING
A grocery store

# FORTY MINUTE FINISH

*(Two mop buckets. Two mops. Two guys in smocks.)*

IKE. They're still out there. What the hell could they be talkin' about? The ambulance pulled out of here, what, 7:15. It's like an hour later they're still over there yip yappin away.

TERRY. These things take time I guess.

IKE. I'm trying to make out the words but their lips are too small. Like trying to make sense out of flapping bologna. Can you make out anything?

TERRY. No.

IKE. C'mon, look for real. Can you read what they're saying?

TERRY. Maybe. I don't know.

IKE. Oh, hold back, man. Don't astound me with the eagle eyes.

TERRY. It's none of our business.

IKE. When the hands are feeling any part of eight o'clock on a Sunday and I'm still sporting this smock, it's totally my business. *(Looking one last time.)* Hell with it, let's just go.

TERRY. Aren't you gonna help me?

IKE. Help you? Help you what? There's nothing left.

TERRY. We might of missed something.

IKE. Let's inspect. *(To the floor.)* What am I seeing? I'm seeing me. I'm seeing you. I'm seeing us. A reflection. The floor's spotless. What's the problem?

TERRY. I don't know. Feels disrespectful. How old do you think that guy was? Sixty? Sixty-five?

IKE. He was old.

TERRY. Exactly my point. He was old.

IKE. Yeah. And old people have strokes, that's what they do.

TERRY. But they usually don't crack their heads open in the process. I mean, you think he's dead?

IKE. I don't know. How would I know?

TERRY. What I'm saying is, people bleed, yeah. But to see it like that. To watch his life spread down the aisle. Somethin' about it. Just didn't seem ... Human, you know?

IKE. Well, humans bleed. That's what they do.

TERRY. How can you be like that?

IKE. How am I like, Terry?

TERRY. This is something here. What me and you witnessed.

IKE. We really didn't see anything. He was on the floor before we got here.

TERRY. So, it doesn't bother you?

IKE. What do you want? You want me to squirt a few? I didn't even know the man.

TERRY. You know how long it took to clean up?

IKE. What's that have to do with anything?

TERRY. Forty -two minutes.

IKE. It was longer than that.

TERRY. Forty-two I checked the clock.

IKE. And you're callin' me distracted?

TERRY. 7:32 we started. First change of water 7:46. Last change eight o'clock. Bringing us up to now. The water's hardly red. Forty minutes. To clean up sixty-year-old blood.

IKE. It was a pain.

TERRY. That can't be possible, right?

IKE. Like a tipped stack of egg cartons.

TERRY. To erase somethin' that old that quick. There's something wrong in that, isn't there?

IKE. You want to give it another once over, what?

TERRY. You're missing the point.

IKE. No, I'm missing the game. And I can't punch out until you do. So if it's going to take us sliding the mop fifty times more, then let's do it.

TERRY. You have to know what I'm talking about.

IKE. What is it we're supposed to do? Turn the clock. Split inside the guy and fix his stroke? We're here to bag groceries. To mop the floors. Not place a Band-Aid on the order of the fucking universe.

TERRY. I just feel we have to own up to the event somehow.

IKE. Did we do it? Did we slam his head into the tile?

TERRY. We cleaned up.

IKE. So that's supposed to tie a knot between us and this guy. You even know this guy's name? I can hardly remember what the man was wearing and I'm supposed to light a candle right here in the middle of the bread aisle.

TERRY. What *was* he wearing?

IKE. Huh?

TERRY. I can't remember what he was wearing.

IKE. Who cares?

TERRY. Somebody does. Somebody's going to want to know what he looked like right before he ... you think he's dead?

IKE. Maybe. Who knows. And if he is, what can you do?

TERRY. I could've paid attention. I mean, I would've never noticed the guy at all if he didn't hit the floor. That's all I'm going to remember.

IKE. That's all you can remember. Look, you're tired. You're freaked. But it's over.

TERRY. Yeah. Finished.

IKE. Let's go, huh? We'll watch the game. Throw a few down. Sleep solid. What do you say?

TERRY. Something just won't let me move, you know. Feel like something should be said.

IKE. *(Pause.)* Brown pants. Grey sweater. Baby Blue zigzags.

TERRY. What's this?

IKE. What he was wearing.

TERRY. You remember what he looked like?

IKE. Yeah. Black dude. Grey beard. Kinda looked like Grady from *Sanford and Son.*

TERRY. *(Small laugh.)* Get outta here.

IKE. He did. Spittin' image. Almost asked for an autograph when he first stepped in.

TERRY. You know, it is possible. You think it might've been him?

IKE. Nah.

TERRY. Stranger things have been known to happen. You don't think that there's even a chance?

IKE. Nah.

TERRY. You really think he's dead?

IKE. *(Pause.)* Yeah. *(Silence.)* Punch the clock for ya?

TERRY. Sure. *(Pause.)* Some night, huh?

IKE. Some night.

*(Fade.)*

**END OF PLAY**

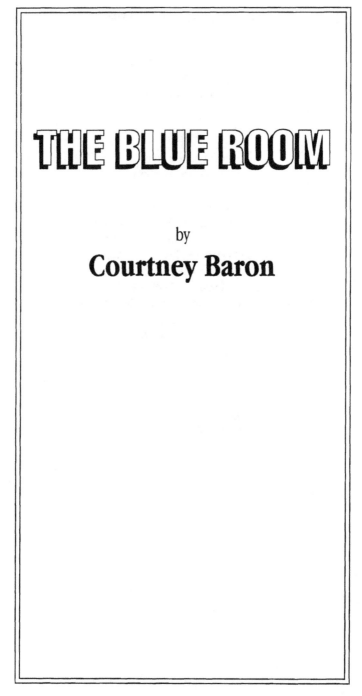

# THE BLUE ROOM

by

## Courtney Baron

## THE BLUE ROOM
### by Courtney Baron
Directed by Maria Mileaf

### CAST
*Woman:* Carla Harting
*Sailor:* Bruce McKenzie

Scenic Designer: Paul Owen
Costume Designer: Michael Oberle
Lighting Designer: Mimi Jordan Sherin
Sound Designer: Darron L. West
Properties Designer: Mark Walston
Stage Manager: Heather Fields
Assistant Stage Managers: Dyanne M. McNamara,
Alyssa Hoggatt
Dramaturgs: Amy Wegener, Sara Skolnick
Casting: Laura Richin Casting

### SETTING
The middle of the South Pacific,
coordinates: 48° 30′S/125°30′W

# THE BLUE ROOM

*(Lights up. The middle of the South Pacific, coordinates: 48° 30´S/ 125° 30´W. A blue room rocks steadily, twilight casts shadows of waves on the walls. A WOMAN in a blue slip lightly drags her finger in a blue tub of water, moving a tiny blue toy boat. A SAILOR kneels on the upper deck of his ship, looking out into the ocean. He scrubs the deck with a brush. He remembers the WOMAN, she remembers nothing but the moment of his memory.)*

SAILOR. She dreams of me.

*(The WOMAN dreams.)*

SAILOR. She loves the water.

*(She puts her feet into the tub and smiles.)*

SAILOR. She loves the water, I think sometimes she may be a seal. I can picture her smiling, lips pulled back and I see her teeth, her gums are fleshy like salmon, I think sometimes she is a seal.

*(The WOMAN pours water into the tub.)*

SAILOR. What do you love?
WOMAN. *(Reacting to the water in the tub.)* Water.
SAILOR. She comes to the locks to watch the ship come in. When the salmon spawn they get caught in the locks and seals congregate because the catch is easy, like pink gold. They swat and catch enough to be full in an hour. We men try to keep them at bay but they always return. It's like trying to keep a kid out of a candy store. She says something, something that would make anyone fall in love, but really she just says ...

WOMAN. *(As if she's heard a noise.)* Hello?

SAILOR. And I can't help myself because she would make a good catch for any man. And I don't know anything about her before the ship comes in and we're married before I set sail again. She dies while I'm away and I remember her into the sea. And without knowing it, she's trapped in the blue room where we spent our first night together. I trap her there with too much remembering. And as the tale goes, the sailor who remembers love too strongly, who thinks of her too hard will find nothing but the woman trapped in the memory, out to sea, in the middle of the sea. Too far for anyone to swim safely and there are no seals out here.

*(The SAILOR jumps ship. He lands on the periphery of the blue room.)*

SAILOR. *(Continuing.)* Just the blue motel room. And she tells me she loves the water, and I tell her I will have to leave and she tells me she married me because she loves the sea and wants me to take her along. But I can't and she tells me I'm her last chance. And I say that chance is never worth depending on and when I leave in the morning, she spits and says that she will get there one way or another. And so she does. Because she is well versed in the game of memory. In the lore of sailors. And in the middle of the sea she gets what she wants without begging. And I sail for money, because it is a job. Because the ocean is only the traveling—land is the arrival. And she loves the water. She loved me, maybe. Married me, to be out at sea, where land is a memory, I think she is a seal.

*(The SAILOR enters the blue room.)*

WOMAN. Here is my sailor.
SAILOR. She is my wife.

*(The SAILOR slides into the tub. The WOMAN giggles.)*

WOMAN. I'll give you a bath, it's what a dirty sailor needs, wash the grit. *(He kisses her and she shies away.)* Look what I've brought you! *(She holds up the toy boat.)* For my sailor! Tell me about the sea.

*(He tries to kiss her again, she laughs and splashes him.)*

SAILOR. Come here.
WOMAN. Tell me about the boat, the sails ...

SAILOR. It's cold and lonely and smells of fish.

WOMAN. Ha! My sailor!

SAILOR. We spend the days barefoot, socks mold to our feet if we leave them on while we work.

WOMAN. You've made the sea here, taste the water. From the salt between your toes.

*(She washes him with a cloth in the tub.)*

SAILOR. You can't drink sea water.

WOMAN. I know of a place where you can, just where it feeds into the Amazon, off the coast of South America, in the Atlantic a hundred miles before the shore, the water there is fresh, you must have been there.

SAILOR. No.

WOMAN. No?

SAILOR. No.

WOMAN. I would go there and drink the ocean. Like the story of the five Chinese brothers, all identical, with different talents. The first brother could swallow the entire ocean. Hold it all in his mouth. Full and smiling. I would be full and smiling if I drank the ocean.

SAILOR. You would dehydrate and die.

WOMAN. Have you ever washed behind your ears?

SAILOR. I'll buy you a house. You can fill it with flowers.

WOMAN. Buy me a boat, I'll be happy then.

SAILOR. There are no flowers on boats. It's bad luck to bring them aboard. Nothing grows there but moss and longing.

WOMAN. My father was a farmer, the only thing he grew was dirty root vegetables, potatoes and turnips, he died and I said I would never grow a damn thing. So, I came to coast, everything is under the surface of the water ... I never learned to swim and the first time I saw the sea I knew I didn't need to know how.

SAILOR. You have to swim, to be a sailor, you have to.

WOMAN. My father found nothing but bitterness in the ground.

SAILOR. When I'm at sea, do you know what I think of?

WOMAN. Freedom?

SAILOR. Land. All day I look out to see hard dry earth. I crave it. I've gotten to where sand won't do, I prefer grass, hard dirt. I miss mud. Clean things. A woman to hold onto.

*(He pulls her in close.)*

WOMAN. But at night, do you follow the stars?

SAILOR. Sure.

WOMAN. And see the red meteors?

SAILOR. Mostly we see nothing. Just waves and more waves. The night, the day, the day, the night, the clouds and flying fish. I'm getting out.

WOMAN. What?

SAILOR. Of the bath. Come to bed.

WOMAN. But the water is just right.

SAILOR. Why did you pick me?

WOMAN. Pick you?

SAILOR. A whole crowd of us and you came up to me.

WOMAN. Get back in.

SAILOR. You're beautiful.

*(He stands up, dripping wet, he pulls her close. He looks her in the eyes, she looks above him and then grabs one of his hands.)*

WOMAN. Your hands are like barnacles.

SAILOR. Sailing is my trade, only a job.

WOMAN. Funny, my father's hands were like potatoes, eyed with calluses.

*(He finally kisses her hard and she goes limp. He lays her down.)*

SAILOR. Barnacles make cement, stick to anything they touch, won't let go.

WOMAN. And you won't let go.

SAILOR. In the morning.

WOMAN. Take me with you.

SAILOR. I can't.

WOMAN. I want to live on the ocean.

SAILOR. I'll be back. You have the ring, my promise.

*(She pulls away, stands, back to the SAILOR.)*

WOMAN. Do you know that there is gold in the sea? I want that. I want to be a sailor.

SAILOR. You're a sailor's wife.

WOMAN. I will follow you.

SAILOR. You'll make us a home. We'll have children to keep you company.

*(He hovers over her and kisses her. He starts to undress her.)*

WOMAN. I picked you because I could smell it on you, see it in your watery eyes, I knew that you would love me enough to want—

SAILOR. I want you on the shore.

WOMAN. —to take me with you.

SAILOR. I became a sailor because I had nothing to come home to. And if you come with me, what then?

WOMAN. You'll be home.

*(The WOMAN pulls away.)*

SAILOR. No. It moves too much. No matter what you've heard, everyone gets sick. You'd get sick. All of that damned back and forth, everything gets lost. Your sense of taste, of smell. Everything. And your skin never feels right.

*(They exchange a look, the WOMAN seems to resolve something, she falls back into the SAILOR's arms.)*

WOMAN. Then you'll dream of me and I will follow you.

*(The SAILOR closes his eyes. He returns to the deck of the ship and resumes his scrubbing. He speaks while the WOMAN does the following: The WOMAN returns to the position she was in at the start of the play. She replays her movements from the beginning until the point of the SAILOR's entry: The WOMAN dreams. She puts her feet into the tub and smiles. The WOMAN pours water into the tub.)*

SAILOR. The night, the day, the day, the night, the clouds and the flying fish. She died the afternoon I left. They sent word and I dreamt of her. I put her out to sea. And at the point in the South Pacific where land is farthest away on both sides, the blue room appeared. I passed it once, I knew she was there. But she is stuck in the memory and doesn't know that I have given her a home on the open sea. Rocking back and forth. Her skin is slick now from the mist and waves. Her hands are like nothing and I try to remember her differently, give her something else, to let her know that I have given her the sea and I have no reason to touch land again. I think maybe she is a seal, stuck in the blue room where we spent our wedding night. And it floats there.

*(The SAILOR jumps, the sound of splashing water.)*

WOMAN. Here is my sailor. *(The SAILOR slides into the tub. The WOMAN giggles.)* I'll give you a bath, it's what a dirty sailor needs, wash the grit. *(He kisses her and she shies away.)* Look what I've brought you! *(She holds up the toy boat.)* For my sailor! Tell me about the sea.

*(He tries to kiss her again, she laughs and splashes him.)*

**END OF PLAY**

# LABOR DAY

by

## Sheri Wilner

**LABOR DAY**
**by Sheri Wilner**
Directed by Abby Epstein

### CAST
*One:* Nick Garrison
*Two:* Erica Blumfield
*Three:* C. Andrew Bauer
*Four:* Monica Koskey
*Five:* Bryan Richards
*Six:* Carolyn Baeumler

Scenic Designer: Paul Owen
Costume Designer: Michael Oberle
Lighting Designer: Mimi Jordan Sherin
Sound Designer: Darron L. West
Properties Designer: Mark Walston
Stage Manager: Heather Fields
Assistant Stage Managers: Dyanne M. McNamara,
Alyssa Hoggatt
Dramaturgs: Michael Bigelow Dixon, Ilana Brownstein
Casting: Laura Richin Casting

### CHARACTERS
ONE, male or female, age 21-28
TWO, male or female, age 21-28
THREE, male or female, age 21-28
FOUR, male or female, age 21-28
FIVE, male or female, age 21-28
SIX, female age 29

### TIME & PLACE
The night before Labor Day, 11:50 p.m. A party.

# LABOR DAY

*(Labor Day Eve, 11:50 p.m. A nondescript room, save for some white decorations and furnishings. Six friends, all dressed completely in white, sit in a circle. Characters ONE, TWO, THREE, FOUR and FIVE range in ages from 21 to 28. Character SIX is 29.*
*They are playing a party game and strike their chests with their hands before speaking.)*
*(AUTHOR'S NOTE: Although individual directors and casts are encouraged to create their own way to play the fictional game, a particularly effective method was discovered for the Actors Theatre of Louisville production. After each player called out a word and hit his or her chest, the other players, one at a time in counterclockwise order, would hit their chests, as well. The next word was not called out until a complete round of "chest-hitting" had been completed. The method created a ritualistic rhythm and set a good speed for the game.)*

ONE. *(Hits chest.)* Sale.
TWO. *(Hits chest.)* Noise.
THREE. *(Hits chest.)* Pages.
FOUR. *(Hits chest.)* House.
FIVE. *(Hits chest.)* Collar.
SIX. On rice.
ALL. One word!
SIX. Close enough.
ONE. It is not. No way.
THREE. And you didn't tap your chest.
SIX. *(Hits chest.)* On rice.
FOUR. It's not one word and you didn't tap your chest.
SIX. *(Hits chest repeatedly to get a "reverb" effect.)* O-o-o-o-n-n-n r-i-i-i-c-c-c-e.
FIVE. You're out.
SIX. It's just a game.

FIVE. Right. And you lost it. Sit over there.

SIX. It's my white party and I'll sit where I want to. Sit where I want to. Sit where I want to.

*(They watch her in silence as she chooses a location for herself. It is off to the side and near a white table covered with an array of white foods.)*

ONE. Actually, it's my white party.

SIX. Obviously. If it were my WHITE party, I wouldn't serve WHITE wine.

FIVE. *(Hits chest.)* Wine.

SIX. White wine is white in name only.

ONE. *(Hits chest.)* Head.

TWO. *(Hits chest.)* Out.

THREE. *(Hits chest.)* Face.

SIX. Anyone want more Wonder Bread balls? Popcorn? Milk?

ALL. No.

*(They continue with their game, ignoring her while she speaks.)*

FOUR. *(Hits chest.)* Russian.

SIX. *(Shrugs.)* More for me. *(SIX pours herself a glass of milk. She raises her glass.)* Here's snow in your eye. *(She drinks.)*

FIVE. Wash.

ONE. Wedding.

TWO. Meat.
THREE. Fish.
FOUR. Cap.

FIVE. Christmas.

SIX. What will you miss the most?

Me, I'll miss the danger. The terror felt at every forkful, at the possibility that a dozen dots of marinara will spray onto your chest. Or that a fist size clump of chocolate ice cream will lean off its cone and fall right into your lap.

ONE. Lines.

TWO. Chocolate.
THREE. *(Hits chest.)* Guilt.
FOUR. *(Hits chest.)* Man.

SIX. No, you can never feel safe wearing white. That's what I'll miss, believe it or not.

FIVE. Wall.

SIX. Somehow, it makes you more sensitive. More awake. More aware of every wave pattern in the atmosphere. Is that a rain

ONE. Bread.

SIX. cloud? A sticky-fingered child? Do I look like a nurse? My period was last week, right? In white, all your senses are

TWO. Castle.

SIX. heightened. You hear new sounds, smell more smells. You develop a whole new set of senses.

FOUR. *(Hits chest.)* Slavery.

FIVE. *(Hits chest.)* House.

ALL. Said it!

FIVE. No sir.

ONE. Yes sir.

FIVE. No way!

THREE. Oh please, of course someone said White House.

FIVE. Who did?

FOUR. I did.

FIVE. I didn't hear you.

ONE. I heard her.

FIVE. Well I didn't.

FOUR. I definitely said White House.

FIVE. When?

SIX. *(Hits chest.)* Sale. *(Hits chest.)* Noise. *(Hits chest.)* Pages. *(Hits chest.)* House. Fourth item called. Then *(Hits chest.)* collar, then the fatal *(Hits chest.)* on rice.

FOUR. *(To FIVE.)* Have a seat.

FIVE. I thought she said mouse.

ONE. *(Hits chest.)* Mouse.

TWO. *(Hits chest.)* Album.

THREE. *(Hits chest.)* Lie.

*(FIVE walks over to the food area. SIX offers FIVE a glass.)*

FOUR. Trash.

SIX. Milk?

ONE. Race.

FIVE. No thanks. *(FIVE pours a glass of white wine.)*

TWO. Flag

SIX. You're better off. It's a stupid game. Limited to one

THREE. Tie.

word. How much is neglected
because of that punishingly
arbitrary rule? *(She hits her
chest.)* Cliffs of Dover. Hills
like *(She hits her chest.)*     FOUR. Flight.
elephants.
FIVE. *(Hits his chest.)* men     ONE. Knight.
can't jump.
SIX. That's actually not one      TWO. Owl.
I''ll miss.
FIVE. Ha! That's a good one!      THREE. Supremacists.
FIVE. *(Cont./ Hits chest.)*
Men can't jump. Hey, is
there any more vanilla ice
cream left?

                                  FOUR. Lightning.

ONE. In the freezer.    Fang.
FIVE. Excellent                   TWO. Diamonds
*(FIVE starts to exit.)*
SIX. Wait!                        THREE. Sox.
FIVE. What?                       FOUR. Haired.
SIX. Tell me what you'll          ONE. Rabbit.
miss. The most. About
wearing white.
FIVE. I never wear white.         TWO. Water.
This party every year is the
only time I ever do. *(FIVE
exits.)*
SIX. *(To group.)* Did you
hear that? *(Yelling after       THREE. Light.
FIVE.)* You're not invited
next year.
TWO. *(Hits chest.)* Market.
THREE. What the hell's a *(Hits chest.)* market?
TWO. I don't know. There's a black market. That means there
must be a *(Hits chest.)* market, right?
ONE. No.
FOUR. Buh-bye.
TWO. Who's got a dictionary?
ONE. I do. But it's red.
THREE. Buh-bye.
TWO. Shit

*(TWO sits down next to SIX. SIX offers TWO a bowl.)*

SIX. Mashed potatoes?

FOUR. Hot.

TWO. Yeah. Thanks. *(TWO takes the bowl and a fork and begins eating.)* Any salt?

ONE. Squall.

SIX. Need you ask? *(SIX hands TWO a salt shaker.)* What will you miss the most? About wearing white?

THREE. Pride.

FOUR. Sauce.

ONE. Mountains.

TWO. *(Thinks for a moment before answering.)* If you don't

TWO. *(Cont.)* have a tan, it looks like you do. If you do have a tan, it looks even darker.

THREE. Plains.

FOUR. Rat.

SIX. I'll miss the possibilities. There's nothing quite like that giddy post-Memorial Day moment when you open up your closet and think: "Anything. Absolutely anything." There's no reaching for something and then stopping yourself. No fears, no hesitations. You thrust in your hand and can pull anything out. Absolutely anything.

ONE. Satin.

THREE. Pine.

FOUR. Paper.

ONE. Tailed.

TWO. That's not true for me.

THREE. Rage.

SIX. Why not?

FOUR. Space.

TWO. I don't wear red in summer. I could have the greatest tan, but I put on red and some moron inevitably says, "ouch, bad burn."

ONE. Hope.

THREE. Chapel.

THREE. *(Hits chest.)* Gold.

FOUR. *(Hits chest.)* Knuckled.

*(FIVE re-enters.)*

FIVE. You guys know what time it is? It's 11:59. *(Everyone but SIX screams, stands, and then runs around the room retrieving their white bags and backpacks.)* Man, if I didn't go into the kitchen—!

ONE. Oh my god, where's my bag? Who's seen my bag?

TWO. What color is it?

ONE. Very funny. Where is it? Where the hell is it?

TWO. Everyone, quick, get your stuff. Quick.

SIX. *(A quiet pronouncement.)* This year I won't do it.

THREE. You're standing on my strap, move!

SIX. *(Still quietly.)* This year I won't do it.

THREE. Get your stuff, hurry!

SIX. I won't do it. I won't give it up. The danger. The freedom. The possibilities. I won't give it up.

FOUR. You have to.

SIX. Why? Who says that I do? Who's issuing the order?

FOUR. Forty seconds to Labor Day!

ONE. Thirty seconds. On your mark, get set ... GO! *(Suddenly Everyone but SIX starts to take off their white clothes and quickly replaces them with colored clothes.)* Twenty seconds. Watch the clock.

TWO. *(Struggling.)* Shit. This button won't—

THREE. Hurry. Hurry!

FOUR. *(To SIX.)* Come on.

ONE. Ten seconds.

SIX. STOP! *(Time stops. They all freeze, except SIX.)* Why does today feel like the saddest day of the year? It always has. From early on. I died a small death every September. Every first day of school. The feeling that something was over. Something glorious and light and free was over. Why do we follow clocks and calendars? Daylight Savings and New Year's? Why the divisions? Why the markers? Do we really have to make it so obvious that time is passing? That our sisters are now mothers, our parents now grandparents? That the last remnants of our childhood have all but slipped through our fingers? *(Beat.)* I am staying in these clothes. I am staying in these clothes and safe from breast cancer and ovarian cancer and all other diseases that ignore the young. My legs will stay smooth with thin, hidden veins. My parents will not turn sixty but stay the age they were when they each took a hand and lifted me over puddles. I will not allow another season to pass. I can't stop that blasted ball dropping on New Year's, but I will stop this.

*(Time re-starts, they all resume changing clothes.)*

ALL. *(Except SIX.)* 10, 9, 8

SIX. Stop it.

ALL. *(Except SIX.)* 7, 6, 5

SIX. I said stop it.

ALL. *(Except SIX.)* 4, 3, 2

SIX. Stop it.

ALL. *(Except SIX.)* Happy Labor Day!!

*(They cheer, yell, hug and blow noisemakers.)*

SIX. EVERYBODY STOP IT!!

*(They stop what they are doing and stare blankly at SIX. On her hands and knees, she moves about the room gathering all of their white clothes, and in the press, one of the white balloons. She holds the clothes tightly to her chest and buries her face in them. Pause.)*

FOUR. It's just pants and shoes. You can still wear white shirts.
ONE. Yeah, and there's always winter whites.
SIX. None of you know. None of you have any idea.
        *(Hits chest.)* I miss the freedom.
        *(Hits chest.)* I miss the freedom.
        *(Hits chest.)* I miss.

*(SIX releases the white balloon and watches it float up into the air.)*

**END OF PLAY**

CPSIA information can be obtained
at www.ICGtesting.com
Printed in the USA
LVHW041131160919
631186LV00020B/482/P